Better Homes and Gardens®

baths

Meredith® Books
Des Moines, Iowa

Better Homes and Gardens® Baths
Editor: Paula Marshall
Project Manager: Catherine M. Staub, The Lexicon Group
Contributing Editors: Julie Collins and Dave Remund, The Lexicon Group
Graphic Designer: David Jordan
Copy Chief: Terri Fredrickson
Publishing Operations Manager: Karen Schirm
Senior Editor, Asset and Information Manager: Phillip Morgan
Edit and Design Production Coordinator: Mary Lee Gavin
Editorial Assistant: Kaye Chabot
Book Production Managers: Pam Kvitne, Marjorie J. Schenkelberg, Rick von Holdt, Mark Weaver
Contributing Copy Editor: Ro Sila
Contributing Proofreaders: Dan Degen, Kathi DiNicola, Sara Henderson
Cover Photographer: James Yochum Photography
Indexer: Kathleen Poole

Meredith® Books
Executive Director, Editorial: Gregory H. Kayko
Executive Director, Design: Matt Strelecki
Executive Editor/Group Manager: Denise Caringer
Marketing Product Manager: Tyler Woods

Publisher and Editor in Chief: James D. Blume
Editorial Director: Linda Raglan Cunningham
Executive Director, New Business Development: Todd M. Davis
Executive Director, Sales: Ken Zagor
Director, Operations: George A. Susral
Director, Production: Douglas M. Johnston
Director, Marketing: Amy Nichols
Business Director: Jim Leonard

Vice President and General Manager: Douglas J. Guendel

Better Homes and Gardens® **Magazine**
Editor in Chief: Karol DeWulf Nickell
Deputy Editor, Home Design: Oma Blaise Ford

Meredith Publishing Group
President: Jack Griffin
Executive Vice President: Bob Mate

Meredith Corporation
Chairman and Chief Executive Officer: William T. Kerr
President and Chief Operating Officer: Stephen M. Lacy

In Memoriam: E.T. Meredith III (1933-2003)

All of us at Meredith® Books are dedicated to providing you with information and ideas to enhance your home. We welcome your comments and suggestions. Write to us at: Meredith Books, Home Decorating and Design Editorial Department, 1716 Locust St., Des Moines, IA 50309-3023.

If you would like to purchase any of our home decorating and design, cooking, crafts, gardening, or home improvement books, check wherever quality books are sold. Or visit us at: bhgbooks.com

contents

1

explore the options

Creating the perfect space to begin and end the day starts with a list of your needs and your desires, and the opportunities to meet both. »

>> To create a bath that both serves its functional role and offers a personal retreat is a tough test, and the most common request. Add to that the challenge of accommodating the needs of two or more people. Don't despair. Your lessons for success start here. Consider your current and future needs. Do you require a hardworking family bath that withstands daily splashes? Do you want a tranquil space to unwind?

assess your needs

Establishing clear goals for a new bath is the key to successful design. Set primary goals by determining how each person will use the space. The more precise the goals, the more likely the final design will meet expectations. Start by taking detailed stock of the present bathroom situation. Consider everything from materials to the fundamental issues such as layout and fixture location. Perhaps installing new flooring, wall coverings, countertops, cabinetry, or fixtures will solve its problems. Or maybe rearranging the bath's layout so it will better meet the needs of its primary users will do the job.

If those options don't solve the dilemmas, more work—adding on to the existing bath or creating an entirely new bath—may be required. Whatever your needs, balance them against the budgetary bottom line. Later in this book you'll get a financial picture of a bath remodeling. For now, just remember to keep your form and function planning decisions in touch with your financial realities.

OPPOSITE: Designed to promote a sense of tranquility, this master bath also has features that allow two people to enjoy the space simultaneously. A stainless-steel soaking tub was customized to fit two bathers—one end contoured to accommodate sitting up and the other end sloped for reclining.

ABOVE: Even a compact powder room can be functional and stylish. This 5×6-foot room includes a tapered vanity with a small drawer stocked with convenience items for guests. A hand-crafted, sand-cast, white-bronze basin serves as the focal point.

create a wish list

Everyone starts and ends their days with a trip to the bathroom. That room, however, is often stylistically and spatially neglected: It's usually a few functional plumbing fixtures tucked into an exceptionally small room—not exactly a mood brightener!

For your bathroom building project, think beyond the basic box. Bathrooms can be open to the sun and the sky, a favorite garden, or a morning coffee bar. Match the style to the personalities of its daily users, not to what you think a few visitors might expect to see. Keep track of even the most far-fetched ideas. Clever thinking might provide you with the perfect way to include your dream features.

This book is designed to guide your dreams toward creating a workable plan, whether that involves incorporating a soothing whirlpool tub or adding a powder room for convenience.

Inspiration is in every photograph, and practical advice moves you through the planning process on every page. So draw a hot bath, toss in a rubber ducky for company, and flip through these pages to begin imagining your project.

ABOVE: The bathroom is the most personal room in the house, so make it a place you like to be. This well-furnished master suite includes a fireplace wall and raised tub surrounded in marble that extends to the fireplace. Add special accessories such as candles and bath oils to create a feeling of comfort. Include a few things to personalize the space: artwork, music, or a favorite scent. Of course, include fixtures and features that suit your bathing needs and preferences.

OPPOSITE: To complete the spa experience at home, make space for a tempting tub in your bath plans. This one, cradled in a slate surround with limestone border tiles, invites bathers to indulge in daily escapes.

finding

inspiration

You may be updating your existing bath for practical reasons: Dated plumbing fixtures barely function, or an addition to the family has overextended an already cramped bathroom. Perhaps the desire to indulge in a more luxurious bathroom with pampering amenities is driving your remodeling plans. Whatever your reasons, before choosing the plumbing fixtures, even before setting the budget, think about style. After all, once all those practicalities enter the picture, truly indulgent thoughts are overshadowed by facts and figures. You needn't be overly specific, just think of the images and words that convey the abiding intent of your bathroom project: a pampering retreat, a spa at home, soothing colors, quiet repose, traditional elegance, contemporary drama—whatever suits you. Use your style as the inspiration to guide all the choices you'll make in creating your plan.

Think of your favorite things for inspiration. Perhaps it's a favorite travel destination, piece of artwork, or hobby such as gardening.

Be selective. Make a list of your favorite things, colors, materials, and amenities, and then pare down the list. Narrowing your choices doesn't limit your options; it helps you create a unified space.

Be realistic. Whether creating an entirely new space or revamping an old one, consider the bathroom's layout from the floor up. If a palatial master suite with separate toilet compartment, walk-in steam shower, soaking tub made for two, dressing area, and dual vanities are your inspiration but you otherwise adore your one-bedroom bungalow, tailor your desires to suit your space. Work with a design professional to make the most of your space without compromising minimum clearances. Minimum clearances ensure less banging of elbows and doors. Remember storage: Because there never seems to be enough, figure out what you need—and then add plenty more wherever space allows.

OPPOSITE: **Relive travels to favorite destinations without leaving home. This master bath—featuring an eye-catching tub, French doors, multiple rooms, and freestanding furniture—was inspired by the homeowner's stays in French hotels.**

ABOVE: **The original architecture of this 1929 Italianate villa set the tone for this bathroom. The whirlpool tub deck is formed from Italian marble that extends into the shower to create a bench. Arches in the bath echo architecture throughout the home.**

A Soft Touch. Include a stack of extra-thick towels that feel good on the skin to complete the ambience of any bath and create a spa-style retreat at home.

Add a heated bar to hang them on and you'll always have a toasty towel ready when you step out of the tub or shower. Hang a monogrammed terry robe on a nearby bath hook to complete your better-than-any-day-spa retreat.

LEFT: A professional design and architecture team made the homeowners' vision of a quiet, tranquil space a reality in this master bath. Organic materials such as rift-cut white oak for the vanity, honed limestone for the walls, and earthy slate for the floor provide texture.

ABOVE: Look to the existing space for inspiration. A vintage-style bathtub emphasizes the shape of the window bay. The monochromatic color scheme—with subtle variations of color on the walls, woodwork, and cabinets—visually enlarges the space.

suit your style

2

More than a space for mundane grooming tasks, a renovated bathroom can be an expression of your style and pamper your needs. »

>> Just as a long soak in a luxurious whirlpool tub eases tired muscles, your bathroom should offer a look that relaxes and renews—whether you're waking up to start the day or winding down after hours on the run. Surround yourself with colors, textures, materials, and accessories that make you comfortable, happy, and relaxed. A successful bathroom makeover comes from making choices you will enjoy each day.

contemporary

The gallery of ideas in this chapter provides myriad ideas for bathroom styles. Each one was designed to meet the personal needs and interests of the homeowners. As you peruse each layout, take note of what you like as well as what you don't like. Knowing what you do not like is just as important in achieving your ideal bath as articulating what you want to include.

If you are uncertain about what look is right for you and your family, touring this gallery of ideas is an excellent starting point. Remember that the bath is your personal space—mix and match, borrow from, and combine the looks you see here to create a room uniquely yours.

To create a soothing, spalike retreat, for example, choose serene colors and tile or stone finishes with a smooth, polished look. If textured warmth is more your idea of comfort, make room for a terry-covered stool and an antique-look, furniture-style vanity.

OPPOSITE: **Nature itself becomes part of the contemporary decor by incorporating walls of windows, with frosted glass on the lower panels to provide privacy.**

ABOVE: **Curlicue-shape chrome fixtures lend personality to the bath. Though stylish, some unique-shape handles may be more difficult to turn.**

Contemporary style is known for its clean, straight lines; wood finishes; and appreciation for modern artistry. This style can also be meditative in its calm, quiet attitude. When you think about it, contemporary style is a natural for the bath, where surfaces are sleek and uncluttered, cabinets and countertops are made of wood and natural stone or tile, and opportunities abound for metal accents in hardware and fixtures.

Contemporary-style bathrooms have the following elements in common:

- Wood-tone built-in cabinets with flat door and drawer fronts. You won't find recessed panels and intricately carved molding in contemporary baths.
- Stone slabs or tiles, such as slate, limestone, granite, or marble.
- Shapely faucets for the tub and shower, and sink.

To Whirl or Not to Whirl? Many new contemporary-style bathrooms feature soaking tubs rather than whirlpools. Soothing sore muscles or frazzled nerves in a bubbling tub is definitely appealing, but will you take the time to use it? If not, you may be better off with a smaller soaking tub or roomy steam shower. Keep in mind that large whirlpool tubs take a long time to fill, are often noisy, and may require added structural support because they are extremely heavy when filled. You may also need a larger (or second) hot water heater to fill the tub while keeping the hot water flowing to other rooms in the house. If a whirlpool is a must-have in your new bath, make sure you insulate the room for sound and/or spend the extra money for a quieter model.

- Built-in, hidden storage, including an appliance garage to conceal hair dryers and electric toothbrushes. Avoid clutter.
- Undermount sinks and tubs that create clean horizontal surfaces.
- Simple metal knobs and pulls.
- Glass shower doors.
- Hard window treatments, such as shutters, blinds, shoji screens, or frosted glass for privacy and light control.

Decorate your bath in a contemporary style, and you'll envelop yourself in a restful retreat.

OPPOSITE: **High style doesn't have to mean high price. These cabinets are modest maple laminate.**

ABOVE: **Slate tiles create an organic pattern on the walls of the open shower and bath tub area.**

traditional

Traditional style turns an ordinary bath into a sanctuary fit for royalty. Whether it's a tiny first-floor powder room or an expansive master bath, a room dressed in tradition possesses an air of graciousness, elegance, and timelessness. This ambience can be reflected in the shape of a faucet handle or the way a drapery graces a window. Inspired by European opulence of the 18th century, traditional style is known for gilded finishes and floral fabrics, as well as enduring accents such as porcelain, gold, and silver. Uncluttered yet sumptuous, it is a statement of luxury, transforming a plain bath into a room from an earlier time.

Achieve a traditional-style bathroom by incorporating the following elements:

- Wood, wood-tone, or white-painted cabinets and furniture.
- Furniture-style vanities, characterized by an elevated bottom edge and exposed legs.
- Freestanding storage pieces, such as armoires and étagères.
- Recess panels and moldings on doors, cabinet fronts, wainscoting, and tub surrounds.
- Architectural details, such as deep molding and windows with muntins.
- Natural surface materials such as stone and tile.
- Wall-mount mirrors framed with wood molding.
- Clean-lined and formal window treatments, such as Roman shades, shutters, or tailored swags.

RIGHT: Enclose a tub in its own arched alcove to create a a sense of intimacy in the area. Steps, inset with tumbled marble for skid resistance, provide easy access to the raised tub.

Other touches that reflect traditional style include:

- Abundant floral or toile fabrics in draperies, vanity skirts, and wallpapers. Keep in mind the humidity in a bath can take a toll on fabrics. If your bath will include fabrics and wallpapers, see page 140 to plan for proper ventilation, or save more delicate fabrics for powder rooms where moisture isn't a concern.
- Brass accents with towel rings, faucets, doorknobs, drawer pulls, and mirror frames.
- Botanical prints and old-world reproductions.
- Vintage collectibles.
- Chairs and footstools that are tailored or upholstered in a brocade or other sumptuous fabric.

LEFT: **Create a display space by installing glass shelves in a tub alcove.**

BELOW: **Subtle variations in color can be more interesting—and more pleasing to the eye—than a lot of different hues. This bath combines a limestone basket-weave backsplash, marble countertop, porcelain sinks, and hand-painted mirror frames.**

OPPOSITE: **Add molding to an otherwise modest mirror and console for traditional style.**

Asian inspiration

With the right design and decor, a household bathroom can offer all the ambience and spirit of an Asian spa. Earthy materials and simple style create an aura of quiet reflection.

In the bathroom here, cool mossy colors and gentle lighting help soothe stressed minds while softening the hard edges of dark stone. Two sinks, set into a slate countertop with an extra-high backsplash, set the minimalist tone with clean lines. Two circular mirrors, similar to reflecting pools, hover under a pleasing wall-to-wall arch, while streamlined faucets reinforce the contemporary feel.

Towel bars have been incorporated into the vanity. Towel storage over the radiator treats you to a sumptuously warm dry-off. A shoji screen set above the tub reflects the Japanese influence, as do the lantern-style sconces. The oval tub, surrounded by a field of slate, has a pleasing sculpted quality, and the stone floor is reminiscent of river rock.

RIGHT: **To help emphasize a calming, Asian theme, select light, earthy colors for the walls. Plan sufficient storage for no-clutter decor. The vanity pairs with mirrors and sconces to soften the hard edges of the slate slab. A shoji screen behind the tub can be back-lit to create a warm glow throughout the room.**

continental

accent the arches around the room. Cream-color paint blended with an umber glaze coats the vanity, giving the new piece an antique appearance. European-style faucets complete the look.

For a slightly less formal, but just as luxurious, bath, recreate an English garden indoors. This bath, *opposite*, took its inspiration from fern-pattern wallpaper that sets a natural theme. Rough-cut Texas limestone laid in an irregular pattern mimics a flagstone path. To complete the look, botanical prints adorn the walls and a fern fills a wall niche near the tub.

LEFT: **Create old-world elegance with careful attention to detail. Crystal handles and a paint-glazing technique on the wood age a new vanity and provide continental style.**

TOP RIGHT: **A leaded- and beveled-glass window above the tub lets in natural light and evokes an English garden atmosphere. A collection of 19th-century botanical prints extend the garden theme in this master bath.**

BOTTOM RIGHT: **Antique pieces lend old-world style to this bath. Before bringing old pieces into the bath, plan for proper ventilation and consider how precious the pieces are to you; over time, moisture may damage them, even when the room has adequate ventilation.**

If you long to create a bathroom that looks as though it hasn't changed for decades, consider the great ideas offered by these old-world spaces. To truly maintain the integrity of days gone by, don't allow any contemporary elements into the room—not even recessed lighting. For example, if you're lucky enough to have windows, consider adding diamond-shape grilles to instantly "age" even the newest fenestrations. Paint the grilles silver and rub black glaze on and off the wood slats to mimic a leaded-glass window. Another key to creating old-world style is the use of ceramic tiles on the bathroom walls.

For this room, striking architectural features such as classical arches produce the formal, old-world atmosphere. A textural combination of mossy green relief tiles and Italian marble add interest as well as European appeal. Bullnose tiles

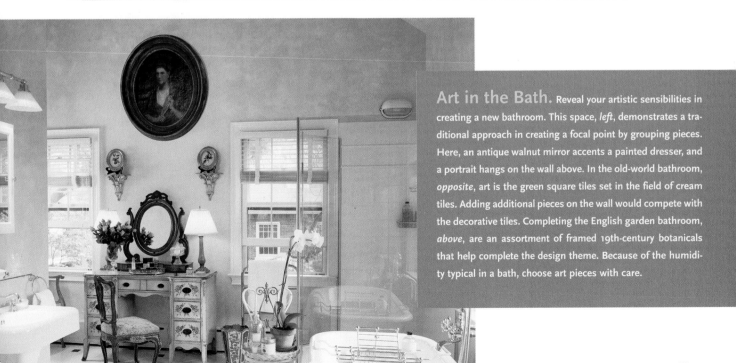

Art in the Bath. Reveal your artistic sensibilities in creating a new bathroom. This space, *left*, demonstrates a traditional approach in creating a focal point by grouping pieces. Here, an antique walnut mirror accents a painted dresser, and a portrait hangs on the wall above. In the old-world bathroom, *opposite*, art is the green square tiles set in the field of cream tiles. Adding additional pieces on the wall would compete with the decorative tiles. Completing the English garden bathroom, *above*, are an assortment of framed 19th-century botanicals that help complete the design theme. Because of the humidity typical in a bath, choose art pieces with care.

arts and crafts

With today's always-on-the run schedules, some people crave simplicity. That may be why the clean lines of Craftsman styling make an especially pleasing choice for master-suite retreats. Concentrating a bathroom plan around grid designs and wide, flat bands of mahogany or painted wood around windows, mirrors, and the tub surround can capture the look. For a cool, restful balance to these warm tones, consider creamy marble or tile flooring.

In the bathroom featured, *right*, crisp Craftsman-inspired lines partnered with an extensive use of white tile and wainscoting reflect the comfortably old-fashioned bath styles of the 1920s. Shiny metal drawer pulls, handles, and accessories such as towel holders and sconces add to the clean metal effect.

LEFT: **Cherry cabinets designed with simple recessed panels and featuring black hardware echo the look of Mission-style furniture common to the Craftsman era.**

ABOVE RIGHT: **Circles, rectangles, the subtle vertical lines of the beaded wainscoting, and planes of solid color all combine in an attractively traditional whole. The molding is wider than normal so it can serve as a ledge for toiletries.**

RIGHT: **Connect a modern convenience— such as this jetted tub—with the rest of the room through the use of a consistent design element; in this example, beaded- board wainscoting. As another modern perk, the underfloor radiant heating system is set to come on an hour before the owners get up each morning.**

colorful

Designing a bathroom is like visiting a salon. Often all you want is a modest makeover—a fresh twist on a favorite style. Sometimes, though, you crave a whole new look—a change so bold that friends won't believe their eyes.

In the contemporary example shown here, two tropical colors—mango and lime—set the tone for the room's striking look. The concrete countertop and some drawer fronts are dyed to fit the overall color scheme, the dye bringing out the sycamore's grain. Round mirrors and shapely sconces help continue the fun feeling. The concrete floor and threshold match the green of the sinks. If such a bold color scheme tempts you, consider whether you'll like the look long-term. Changing this color isn't as simple or inexpensive as repainting the walls.

Color can be effective without being bold. In a more traditional example, *opposite*, a classic blue-and-white color scheme revives a once-dated bath. Crisp white ceramic tile, capped with stacked ceramic moldings, creates a traditional wainscoting around most of the room. The wallpaper above has the same intense color as the collectible china on display throughout the room. Decorative objects that are personally appealing and meaningful lend color to a bathroom, and they can help make a bath feel more gracious and less utilitarian.

RIGHT: **Transform your bath without moving fixtures. Here, the vanity combines sycamore cabinetry with a colored-concrete countertop. Angled fronts on the integral sinks serve a practical purpose by increasing sink volume, and fit the room's geometry.**

LEFT: A concrete floor and dyed sycamore drawer fronts bring out the room's palette of mango and lime. Bold shapes, such as the round mirrors and trapezoidal vanity, play up the bath's contemporary design.

BELOW: Hooks take up less space than towel bars—a smart option in a modest-size bath. Plus, hooks display colorful towels in a more relaxed, comfortable way.

BOTTOM: With the faucet set installed directly into the countertop, the decorated sink looks like another piece of porcelain on display.

natural country

If grand views, a lush garden, or quaint courtyard beckon you outdoors from your bathroom, bring the outdoors in with natural or natural-look materials. To create a mountain-inspired room, bring in the "earth" with Mexican tile floor pavers, textured plaster walls, and a hand-formed concrete countertop and tub surround. In this bath, layered atop the wall from baseboard to wainscot, formed concrete reflects the peaks and valleys of the nearby Sonoma Mountains. Concrete is fairly fluid, so it can be cast in shapes that you can't form with other materials such as granite, which comes in slabs or tile. Consider finishes throughout the room. Here rough-hewn fir beams and a pine ceiling enhance the out-of-doors design.

Position windows to provide the best outdoor views from a vantage point, such as from a soaking tub. Include appropriate window treatments, such as roller shades, that can be drawn for privacy.

OUTDOOR CONNECTION

Any bathroom can benefit from a true connection to the outdoors. This bath-room is linked to a courtyard with French doors, which also bring in abundant sunlight during the day. Keep your outdoor connection private with a courtyard created from wood fencing, brick or stone walls, or a hedge of bushes. Use brick, stone, or stamped-and-colored concrete to form an elegant patio. Finish the mini-oasis with a comfortable chaise where you can kick back and wind down after a hot, relaxing shower or soak in the tub.

LEFT: **Whitewashed fir beams and a pine ceiling enhance the outdoor feel of this naturalistic bath. French doors open to a courtyard. Hand-formed concrete panels surrounding the tub mimic the contours of the nearby Sonoma Mountains that inspired the design of this bath.**

ABOVE: **The custom vanity features a natural, light, distressed finish. The hand-formed concrete backsplash continues around the bathroom walls as a wainscot treatment.**

timeless

treasure

Opposites attract, and the idea is truer when it's expressed in black and white. One of the best aspects of this crisp combination is its ability to add sparkle and modern convenience to a vintage design, an especially favorable approach when updating a bath in an old house.

To blend old and new, try a vintage flooring design of white tile punctuated with black tiles. Because the white and black combination has timeless appeal, you're unlikely to tire of it, or feel it's dated as trends come and go. Tuck a purely contemporary in-floor heating system below the tile to ensure toasty toes whenever you step out of the tub or shower.

Glossy white subway tiles on the walls help to make a small room seem more spacious than its true dimensions. Add a band of black tile at the top of the wainscoting to tie in with the flooring. Reflective surfaces throughout the bath—the glossy tiles, mirrors, glass, polished chrome—all enhance the clean, airy look.

In a small bath such as this one, installing a recessed medicine cabinet above the sink provides storage and contributes to the vintage look.

LEFT: When vanity space is limited, try a small, streamlined sink. The polished chrome frame of this base includes bars that can be used to hold guest towels.

ABOVE RIGHT: Offset a bathroom of hard, smooth tile with a shower curtain that adds soft texture.

RIGHT: A band of white marble tile sandwiched between two small bands of black punctuates the 3x6-inch subway tiles on the wall.

plan your layout

Design an ideal bath space that meets the functional and aesthetic needs of two or more people. »

3

» Planning the layout for your new bathroom involves more than simply fitting in a tub, shower, toilet, and sink. Your bathroom should fit your lifestyle. Whether it successfully meets the needs of your family is in part a matter of its layout, its components, its materials, and its style. In this chapter you'll see how a hardworking bathroom can also be a luxurious master retreat, family-friendly bath, or a welcoming guest respite.

master baths

The overriding trend in today's master bath is to create a soothing retreat at home. The definition of soothing retreat is up to you, of course. During the planning stages, consider amenities such as a steam shower, towel warmers, and under-floor radiant heating that provide spalike comforts. Many master baths also incorporate features that accommodate the needs and preferences of two bathers—for example, a separate shower and bathtub, and separate vanities.

Because two people generally share a master bath, compartmentalizing enables couples to share the bathroom while offering privacy to each person. In these bath plans, separate compartments house the toilet (and sometimes include a bidet and a shower too). This type of plan, however, can be a space-grabber.

RIGHT: A roomy 3¹/²×5¹/²-foot shower will accomodate a wheelchair if necessary. An in-bath linen closet stores towels, grooming supplies, and other necessities.

OPPOSITE: The bath's tile-wrapped surround is wide enough to hold accessories. Large windows let in plenty of natural light.

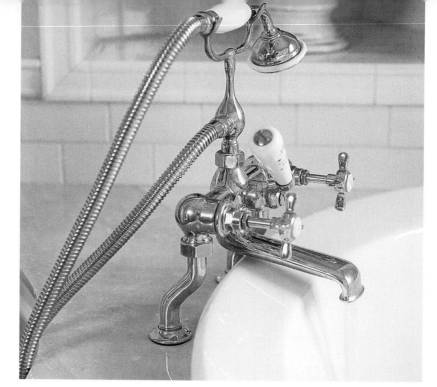

If you don't want to relinquish an entire bedroom to create an elaborate compartmentalized bath plan, you may need to add on to your house. Another option is to scale back plans. Here are less costly solutions that create compartments in a smaller space:

• In a standard-size 5x8-foot bathroom, where the toilet and shower sit just beyond the vanity cabinet, shorten the vanity by a few inches. Then fill in the newly created space with a wall and sliding pocket door to separate the tub and toilet from the vanity.

• Installing a half-wall instead of a full wall isn't as private but saves costs.

• Prefer something even simpler? Set up a folding privacy screen to keep the commode out of view from the other areas of the bath.

LONG-TERM DESIGN

Accessible design is another consideration for long-term livability and enjoyment of a master retreat. The master bath featured on pages 38–39 includes features to ensure the homeowners can remain in their home and enjoy the master bath in future years.

• Three-foot-wide doorways let a wheelchair pass.

• Removable doors allow roll-up use of the vanities. Drawers and plumbing are out of the way.

• Broad, shallow shelves in the storage closet put many items within easy reach of someone seated.

• The shower is big enough for a wheelchair, and for two people if assistance is needed. The entry threshold can be removed for roll-in access.

• Grab bars can be installed directly into the wall; structural reinforcements are already in place.

• Light controls are installed at 3 feet 6 inches above the floor—an easy-to-reach height.

The bath on these pages demonstrates a room can be luxurious and well-appointed without being crammed with amenities. Equipped with the essential elements, the room is simple. Fine materials such as a travertine deck topping a tile-enclosed whirlpool tub, custom dresserlike vanity, and Victorian faucets, lend elegance. The materials, including the antique pine floor crafted from boards quartersawn from the salvaged beams from an early 1900s warehouse, were selected to infuse the bath with a sense of history. A corner bench in the shower offers sit-down comfort. A separate private compartment houses the toilet, providing privacy.

OPPOSITE TOP: **Infuse a bath with historical style. Cross handles, porcelain accents, and satin-nickel curves convey Victorian elegance.**

OPPOSITE BOTTOM: **Add to the spaciousness of a room by installing a glass shower enclosure. Light, neutral tones throughout the bath increase the roomy feel.**

ABOVE: **Plan for easy access to a deep whirlpool tub. The wide, curved travertine deck provides a convenient seat to access the tub and a shelf to hold bath items.**

family
& guest baths

Having a private bathroom for everyone who lives in or visits your house would be ideal. Reality, though, is often limited by space and budget. When contemplating a guest or family bath, make the most of the space you have available.

It takes careful planning to achieve a bathroom that meets your daily needs and also accommodates visitors. In this home, a remodeling effort was in order. Annexing two neighboring closets opened up the bath. A tub-shower combination was replaced by a roomier custom unit on the adjacent outside wall. Relocating the shower made it possible to add a double vanity, and a toilet was positioned across from the basin nearest to the bathroom door. A sliding frosted glass partition gives the option of closing off one basin and the toilet to effect a powder room.

Closets and hallways should also be a consideration. The redesigned closet in this home provides much-needed storage with drawers, shelves, and pivoting towers. It also serves as a pass-through to the bath and works as a dressing room.

ABOVE: **Keep convenience and privacy in mind. In this bathroom, the toilet sits conveniently just inside the entry to the bath. The solid wall between the toilet and the shower provides privacy and serves as a resting place for the sliding glass partition.**

RIGHT: **To reinvent a hallway area, use a series of doors as entryways and walls. Plan openings with care to avoid complex traffic patterns.**

OPPOSITE: **Remodeling made this bath accessible from the bedroom through a closet dressing area. Cube-shape towers swivel out, exposing additional storage space for hanging clothes, *not shown*.**

JACK-AND-JILL PLANS

Is more than one family member slated to use your new bath? You may want to consider a Jack-and-Jill-style floor plan. Divided into three separate rooms, these baths feature two separate vanity rooms with a shared, doored tub and shower, and toilet area.

This style is particularly useful for baths shared by siblings or other family members. Each person walks from his or her own bedroom into his or her own private vanity room. These plans also work for master baths. In a master bath, separate entrances from the same bedroom lead to separate vanity and dressing areas, and the shower and tub space is located in the middle.

GUEST BATHS

If you can afford the luxury of a bathroom dedicated solely to visitors, placing that guest bathroom at the front of the house makes a dramatic first impression. Another ideal location is adjacent to the guest bedroom. Because guest baths are typically small, a glass shower door helps keep the room visually open. Though guests typically won't have much to store in the bath, be sure to include as much storage as possible for towels and personal amenities. Guests will appreciate your thoughfulness.

ABOVE: **Plan for natural light sources. Light enters this bath through windows in the custom shower. The shower features glass doors and fittings that coordinate with the basins.**

RIGHT: **A white basin with satin nickel fittings is mounted to a limestone backsplash. Position a mirrored medicine cabinet over each basin for extra storage.**

OPPOSITE: **Transform a bath from confining to dual-purpose with unconventional ideas, such as this glass partition notched to fit snugly against a wall-mount vanity. Slide the partition open for a roomy master bath; position it closed to create a private powder room separate from the shower and second vanity.**

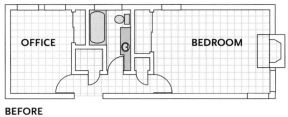

BEFORE

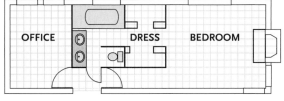

AFTER

small spaces

There are many ways to make your present bath space look, feel, and live larger. To increase floor space, consider replacing a standard-size vanity with a smaller or custom version. The custom pecan vanity shown here follows the curve of the sink, and then steps back to drawers. Frosted-glass doors on the medicine cabinets partially obscure toiletries and contribute to an airy feeling.

To increase storage near a pedestal sink, add a wall-hung medicine cabinet in place of a standard vanity mirror, and then add an 8-inch-wide ledge behind the sink to provide space for makeup and other toiletries.

If your bath is located on an exterior wall, add or increase windows. Windows let in natural light, fresh air, and scenic views while preventing small bath spaces from feeling cramped and claustrophobic.

If you can't squeeze enough space out of the existing bath and adding on is out of the question, look for a more creative solution using space near the bath. Here, removing a ledge next to the old tub-shower unit freed up space for a larger walk-in shower stall. The shower is outfitted with a wall-mount seat that doesn't steal floor space. A clear glass wall and shower door create a seamless effect. Radiant heat flooring in the stall makes the shower warm and inviting.

RIGHT: **Add visual texture to your floor with a blend of complementary colors, such as these black, white, and taupe accent travertine tiles. Maximize once-wasted space near the toilet by installing a single vanity outfitted with below- and above-counter storage. The large walk-in shower with glass doors opens up a visual sweep of the entire space.**

RIGHT: **Consider your options. This once-outdated bath couldn't be enlarged, but the floor plan begged for better space allocation, as well as a sophisticated new look.**

OPPOSITE: **Small doesn't have to mean basic. This walk-in, clear-glass shower stall includes recessed niches, a built-in seat, and showerheads at both ends.**

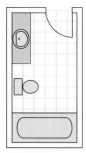
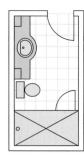

BEFORE   **AFTER**

Small-Space Strategies.

Tiny baths don't need to skimp on style or efficiency. Think outside the box with these tips:

- Sky-High Style. No way to physically expand your space? Fool the eye by emphasizing the room's height with tile, a wallpaper border, or interesting ceiling treatments.
- Go with the Flow. Echo the color scheme used in an adjacent room. When your space is small, it helps to borrow colors and styles from nearby rooms. Keeping the flow continuous makes both rooms feel larger.
- Find a Focal Point. Too much of a good thing can overwhelm a small bath, so limit yourself to one or two signature pieces. Having too many focal points can be distracting.

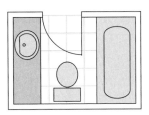

BELOW: Perfect placement is key when square footage is limited. This selection of floor plans for petite bathrooms shows how you can have everything in 75 square feet or less.

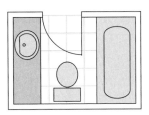

Though it measures only 5x7 feet, this bathroom contains generous counter-top space and base cabinet storage. It would work well for a teen who has lots of grooming supplies.

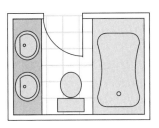

As this floor plan demonstrates, with careful planning, you can fit stylish fixtures into a modestly sized space. Occupying only 48 square feet, the bath contains a generous-size tub and two sinks.

This bath is accessible from both a bedroom and a hallway. To create more clear walkway space, replace the swinging door near the toilet with a pocket door.

ABOVE: Every bathroom needs a focal point. A tile-framed mirror and tile wainscoting make the vanity wall the center of attention. The other lower walls are beaded board, but the same tile cap is used around the room as a unifying design thread.

OPPOSITE TOP: Strive for simple elegance. Here, the claw-foot tub is a reproduction, but the pine floor is a genuine antique, made of salvaged wood. The shower attachment allows a modern bathing option, and the curtain fabric—also used on the French-style bedroom chair—provides the room's strongest dose of color and pattern.

OPPOSITE BOTTOM: A built-in storage niche fits within the bath's clean lines and makes the most of the small space.

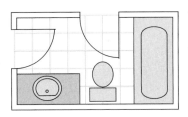

Designed for two people to use simultaneously, this bath has an interior pocket door to create privacy within a limited amount of space. Adding a second pocket door to the wall across from the sinks could create access to another bedroom or hallway.

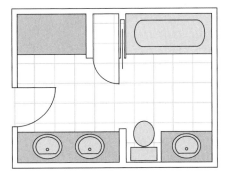

This compartmentalized bath is designed to meet the needs of an entire family.

Treat your guests like royalty by adding a touch of style to the powder room. Whatever your personal style, powder rooms are the ideal rooms to display your preferences. Whether glitz hits the spot or country fits the bill, little extras make a big difference. If your choices seem extravagant, remember that you only need a little bit of anything to fill a powder room.

Shaped sinks with cabinets that angle back are not only elegant, but they also use less precious floor space than standard vanity cabinets. A pedestal sink is a good choice to keep the space open.

Powder rooms are often on high-traffic hallways; that can mean very little privacy and a lot of public inspection from people walking past. The simple amenities of wall and window coverings create a more pleasing view for passersby.

Pocket doors solve the problem of sufficient door swing, and every powder room door deserves a good lock. A partial wall keeps the commode out of view and ensures modesty. Or add a dressing screen to partition the room.

Sometimes the children's bath is the ersatz powder room for guests. If that's the case, consider giving the children an adjacent, separate, vanity area so guests won't have to work around a teen's abundant grooming supplies or wade through a toddler's splish-splash from hand washing.

Budget for good lighting. Not only will your guests appreciate the flattering glow, family members ducking in for a quick primp will like it as well. Wall sconces flanking a mirror convey a cozy, roomlike feel—much better than the harsh shadows cast by a standard-issue ceiling fixture.

powder rooms

LEFT: In a small powder room, a few extras go a long way. Tone-on-tone wallpaper, a decorative paint treatment on the vanity, and a loosely gathered, sheer valance work magic in this narrow powder room.

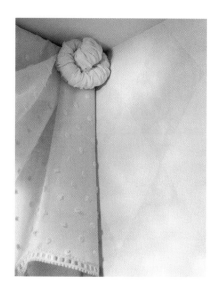

ABOVE: Use fabric to soften the room, particularly because moisture and humidity aren't an issue in powder rooms. The creamy dotted swiss, which blends with the neutral tones of the harlequin-pattern wallpaper, drapes gently from a plump knot at the corner of the valance.

RIGHT: Dress up your powder room. Save money by refurbishing existing fixtures. The dressing-table doors were given a harlequin motif paint treatment and the original wooden countertop received a faux-marble finish.

privacy

If you've never really savored the thought of sharing bath space, consider incorporating two baths into one and enclosing separate toilet compartments. In this bath, a mirror-image vanity divides the bathroom into individual areas—one for each user—while allowing them to see and talk to one another.

The couple prepares for the day about the same time, so they opted for individual bathing fixtures. Each person has an individual shower compartment, separated by a generous-size whirlpool tub for more leisurely bathing. A Botticino marble platform that encases the tub extends into one shower as a handy bench. A 12×12-foot custom translucent, barrel-vaulted skylight and a bank of windows bathe the room in plenty of light. When the afternoon sun becomes too intense, translucent shades provide privacy. The master suite offers two private toilet compartments, one that houses a bidet in addition to the toilet. On one side of the maple vanity, a low counter provides an ideal spot to apply makeup.

OPPOSITE: **An abundance of low cabinetry on both sides of the vanity store grooming aids. At the end is a clothes hamper.**

RIGHT: **The two-sided maple vanity is situated beneath an overhead maple beam that provides a sense of enclosure and coziness. A television above the vanity swivels so that it can be viewed from either side. A pocket door opens to the master bedroom.**

Privacy and Noise Reduction. The bathroom, by its very nature, is a private sanctuary. The people in your family have their own sense of how much privacy they truly need; respect their wishes. Where you reside also has an effect on how much privacy you need. If you live in a secluded area, window coverings may be less of an issue than in the city where a neighbor's window may only be a few feet away. Likewise, narrow horizontal windows placed high on the wall may work well in a second-story suburban bath, but when placed on the first floor, they may put the bath within view of a neighbor's second floor.

Frosted or stained-glass windows provide privacy without blocking out all of the light. Glass block allows in light while obscuring the views. Some blocks distort views and conserve heat better than others, so choose a pattern that makes you feel comfortable. When covering your window with fabrics, avoid thick, heavy fabrics that will soak up moisture. Quick-drying cotton works well, although you may need to line the curtains to avoid transparency. Venetian blinds, vertical blinds, miniblinds, and pull-down shades also work well, while enabling you to control the amount of light that filters into the space.

Like visual privacy, acoustic privacy is also a concern in bathroom design. A ventilating fan can serve as white noise, drowning out the sound of a flushing toilet. Insulating the bathroom walls also helps. Look in home centers for wallboard designed to deaden sound.

dressing rooms

Space planning is often the toughest part of planning a bath project. Existing plumbing lines, chimney flues, and other permanent features of a home may require placing a new bath in an unconventional location or irregular-shape space, or inhibit your plans for updating an existing bath. Fitting in the necessities is difficult enough, much less finding room for the amenities.

Creative thinking about space allows you to add the right kinds of spaces. A dressing room, for example, may seem an amenity. But if fitting in the bathroom basics, adequate closet and dresser space, as well as having sufficient room to get ready to face the day are on your list, including a dressing room may be the answer to meeting your needs.

Part bath, part bedroom, a dressing room takes the space-squeeze off two rooms. In this two-story tract home, the owners knew the only logical place to add a master suite addition was over the garage. Due to the location of the eaves and existing plumbing lines, the new master bath had to serve as the passageway to the bedroom. Making part of the space look more like a hallway and less like a bathroom was a difficult objective.

The solution was dividing the space into a bathroom and a dressing area. The dressing area measures 8 feet wide by 17 feet long—one long wall with a limestone-topped double vanity and two floor-to-ceiling storage cabinets for linen and clothing storage. At the other long side of the dressing area are two built-in dressers and two more floor-to-ceiling storage cabinets.

This arrangement allows for unplanned bonuses: A large skylight welcomes the sun, and the storage keeps the clothing clutter out of the bedroom.

LEFT: A dressing room or area can free up valuable space in the bathroom. This dressing area, beautifully illuminated by clerestory windows, receives light from pendant fixtures and a pair of sconces.

ABOVE: Keep everyday clothing in the dressing room. Built-in drawers are great for that purpose, and tall cupboards are perfect for storing linens and laundry hampers.

storage solutions

Your bathroom should provide a tranquil retreat from the cares of the day. Unfortunately, no matter how well organized you keep the rest of your home, the bathroom can be a natural place for clutter to gather and seemingly multiply. To streamline your morning routine and have a soothing evening ritual, plan for ample storage now to corral the potential clutter before it overwhelms your haven.

OPEN OR CLOSED STORAGE

As you are designing your bath, consider whether you prefer daily-use items out in the open where you can easily view and access them, or if you prefer clean surfaces, clear of all items. Either storage option is fine, just plan your bath accordingly. If you like open storage, install shelves that can hold necessities and display treasures. Locate various-size shelves around the room to hold items just where you'll need them—near the vanity to hold razors and makeup; adjacent to the tub for soaps and shampoo. Incorporating a recessed niche into a shower wall allows for handy storage of shower necessities without the need for additional shower caddies that can take up precious shower space.

If you prefer the idea of clean, unbroken lines and clear countertops, plan for plenty of enclosed storage. A recessed medicine cabinet above the vanity is a standard storage choice, but many new styles offer an even more streamlined appearance than past models. Cabinets below the vanity are another traditional storage choice. Also consider running full-height cabinets from floor to ceiling in one corner of the bath or on both sides of a sink.

OPPOSITE: Install a shelf above a pedestal sink for easy access to frequently used grooming supplies. Place more shelves in other areas of the bath for additional storage and display space.

ABOVE: Install floor-to-ceiling cabinets in your bath for ample storage. Leaving space between the vanity and the corner unit makes the pieces look more like freestanding furniture. To maximize storage potential in the bath, abut pieces.

LEFT: Plan to have a recessed niche installed in the shower or tub area to stow bath necessities.

For more tips on bathroom organization strategies, see pages 142–151.

realize your dreams

Transform your bath vision into an affordable reality. These remodeling strategies show you how. »

» Now it's time to ensure the project fits your budget. Bath remodeling projects fall into at least one of five categories: A facelift involves making cosmetic changes; a renovation encompasses changing the layout within the existing space; an expansion extends an existing bath into adjacent space; a conversion transforms existing square footage to bathroom use; and building an addition is at the top of the cost and complexity scale.

facelift

A bath that works well but looks dated or bland can benefit from an infusion of style. Facelifts include all nonstructural, cosmetic changes, such as repainting or papering the walls, resurfacing walls or tub surrounds, and/or replacing fixtures, flooring, and countertops.

Simple applications of tile or wallpaper, or even a fresh coat of paint and some new hardware, can work miracles, transforming a bland space into a beautiful room.

You can visually enlarge a bathroom by using fool-the-eye techniques. A large wall mirror stretches space by reproducing its image. Glass shower doors let the eye see through a solid surface, preventing the room from being

RIGHT: **Leaves and playful characters on these bas-relief tiles add energy and charm to this room.**

OPPOSITE: **Add life to your bathroom with smart use of color and design. Blue-and-white tiles transform this bath from mundane to magnificent. Create additional counter space by extending the vanity across the top of the toilet.**

chopped into even tinier blocks. A tile frame draws the eye to the window and allows maximum daylight.

As you apply design within your bathroom, add or maintain storage space without sacrificing charm. As shown on page 60, an inexpensive stock vanity can be spruced up using tile. Bottom cabinets remain in place while the top drawer is replaced with a slab of wood and then covered in a matching tile border.

Make your greatest design investments in the focal points of the room. Create continuity, and stay within budget, by using inexpensive white tile for counter, walls, and floor.

An interior designer revamped this bath by covering the dark surfaces with lighter shades and then reworking the existing storage to increase its efficiency.

Wide neutral-stripe paper replaced dark burgundy and navy florals. A border of tumbled marble in soft creams keeps the soft neutral look going. Existing floor and wall tiles were refreshed with a restorative acid wash. The existing dark-stained vanity cabinet was covered with a weathered, warm white paint finish.

Get more storage and function from existing cabinets by making their interior design match individual storage needs. The shallow closet, *left*, once served as barely functional linen storage. The cabinet interior was reworked so that the closet would serve better as a medicine chest. A shallow mirror on the door makes the vanity area appear more spacious and enables the homeowners to get a floor-to-ceiling glimpse of their attire.

If necessary, add freestanding furniture to supplement storage. A freestanding linen storage chest was made to fit into the previously unused space adjacent to the tub in this bath.

ABOVE LEFT: **This shallow storage cabinet was revamped to organize bottles, jars, and tubes instead of linens.**

LEFT: **A coat of white paint and new flower-shape iron drawer pulls update an existing vanity cabinet. Glossy Italian marble replaces the vanity's original countertop.**

RIGHT: **The cleverly hinged shower curtain provides privacy for the tub or shower.**

Renovation goes beyond cosmetic changes to encompass replacing fixtures, changing the layout, adding lighting, enlarging or replacing windows, and making any structural changes short of expansion. Although this remodeling option is typically more costly than a facelift, it can dramatically change the functionality of your bath, possibly making it feel bigger and fit better without adding on to your house.

RELOCATE WALLS

Renovating an existing bath may require removing or adding walls within the existing bath space. Sometimes the floor plan keeps a bath from functioning well. Reconfiguring walls within a bathroom can make that space feel more luxurious for you and your guests.

Imagine your bathroom with a different wall structure. The challenge in this bathroom was making the 7½×11-foot room look larger without changing its dimensions. A wall separated the sink and toilet, and the old tub-shower enclosure crowded the toilet.

Removing the wall between the vanity and toilet opened up the room and allowed the vanity to be widened by 4 inches. The increase was enough so the sink could be moved from the center of the vanity to the far left, allowing for

RIGHT: **A few strokes of design ingenuity help a bathroom live larger and more luxuriously. Here, moving the sink to the far left side of a widened vanity creates more counter space with room for drawers below.**

three dresser-size drawers below the countertop on the right side. More storage was gained by outfitting half of an underused closet with custom cabinets.

Once necessary floor plan changes are made, look to the bath's remaining free space for adding finer touches. The tub-shower combo, with its dated

sliding-glass door, gave way to an open shower-only stall covered in travertine tiles. The same material covers the floor and edges a woven-look limestone pattern on the vanity. Natural stone imparts luxury, and epitomizes style and function—two perfect goals for any bathroom renovation.

renovate

ABOVE: A bath closet is a primary storage space. To get more out of a closet, equip it with custom cabinetry or shelves. Replace wide, unwieldy sliding doors with louvered doors on separate tracks.

LEFT: Think creatively to solve simple challenges. A sink faucet didn't work well with this custom sink—water barely reached the bowl and dripped onto the border. Installing a tub spout did the trick.

GO WITH THE FLOW

Needs change with time, and a dated floor plan can cause challenges and heartache for current-day homeowners. This 13×7-foot bathroom felt and looked cramped. Through renovation of existing space, a separate shower and a double vanity were added without expanding into adjacent rooms.

Often, a few simple shifts can make a room more functional. Here, the original floor plan had the sink and toilet on one wall and the combination tub-shower and two linen closets on another. Moving the toilet to the other side of the room left space for a custom double-sink vanity. A soaking tub now sits across the exterior wall, under the window.

Look for space wherever you can find it. In this room, the side-by-side twin closets gobbled up roughly 21 square feet of floor space. Getting rid of the closets opened up valuable space without losing functionality.

With a new configuration, your old bathroom can take on a whole new life. Here, a glass-enclosed shower on the right fills the spot vacated by one of the closets. A custom cherry armoire took the place of the other. The armoire serves as a medicine chest, so two round mirrors have been mounted above the sinks.

ABOVE: Attention to details will ensure that your bath is both functional and pleasing.

BELOW: This rain-type showerhead delivers a soothing spray of water.

LEFT: A furniture-style vanity provides needed storage space and room for two bowl sinks in this renovated bath.

ABOVE: An armoire replaced a closet, allowing space for a separate tub and shower.

RIGHT: Large floor tiles can help visually expand a small room.

expand

Sometimes the amount of space in an existing bathroom is insufficient, and borrowing square footage from adjoining areas, such as a closet, hallway, or bedroom, is required. Annexing space from an adjoining room solves most problems caused by too-tight dimensions.

If at all possible, look first to closets and other spaces that adjoin your bathroom's "plumbing wall"—the wall that already contains plumbing pipes. It's far less expensive to install fixtures when you can connect them to nearby plumbing lines. Likewise, non-load-bearing walls that have few or no utility lines are much easier and less costly to remove than load-bearing walls with utility lines. If no interior space is available, porches and breezeways are the most cost-effective choices for gaining space.

However you achieve the added square footage, look at the combined spaces as a single new space. Make improvements within the allotted space with smart organization. Tuck built-in dressers close to the walls to maximize floor space. To prevent morning traffic problems, install two sinks in the vanity.

TAKE A LITTLE, GAIN A LOT

Annexing a small amount of space from an adjoining room may have a minimal effect on that room, yet the change may make a major impact on a small bath's functionality. Because bathrooms are often considered little more than a necessity, even some spacious homes have maddeningly tiny baths.

RIGHT: Borrowing from an adjacent bedroom allowed this bath to expand into two halves for added space with privacy to accomodate the needs of a family with three young boys. The boys share two sinks and medicine cabinets, but each has his own set of drawers.

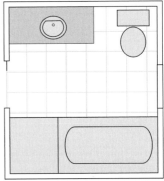

BEFORE

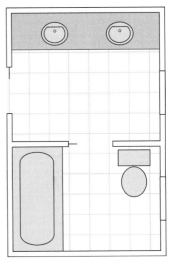

AFTER

ABOVE LEFT: **Countertops should be durable and easy to clean. Add a little fun to the room by personalizing the backsplash or wall with special imprints.**

LEFT: Roll-out steps are a big help to small children, and make great use of limited space. Keep flooring practical, too—such as this ceramic tile.

Designer Tip

If you can't expand over a first-floor roof, consider adding a cantilevered bump-out. Cantilevered bump-outs do not require their own foundation, so they are typically more affordable than additions that require adding on to the home's foundation.

Expanding a bath even minimally can allow for a complete renaissance in style. Open up your bathroom with a bay window and create space for a whirlpool tub with a relaxing view. To complete the new look, match sink faucets with the tub spout. Install hardware pulls and other accents that complement the design of the room. Attention to all the details makes a bathroom remodeling successful.

LEFT: A new bay window bump-out tranformed this bath into a parental retreat.

BELOW: An etched glass door and window in the shower area ensure both privacy and light. A heated slate floor provides warmth on cold mornings.

ABOVE RIGHT: Take inspiration from the main shape or shapes within the room—here curves. Complement the design by selecting sink faucets and spout with high-arc spouts.

RIGHT: Shapely cabinetry pulls and other hand-friendly hardware make for a more inviting experience.

BELOW RIGHT: Natural materials throughout the bath, such as these slate tiles in the shower, instill a tranquil feel.

BOTTOM RIGHT: Curved vanities make it possible to share space without bumping into each other.

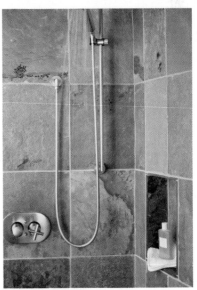

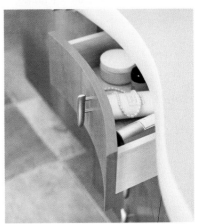

convert
another space

To create an entirely new bath by converting some of your home's existing square footage into a full bath with a tub, toilet, and sink, you'll need a space that measures at least 5×7 feet. If a shower stall is substituted for the tub, the minimum room size can be cut to 3×7 feet. A powder room should be at least 3×6 feet or 4 feet square. (For more information about space requirements, see Chapter 6, "Everything In Its Place," beginning on page 124.)

You may be able to add a new bath to existing square footage, including contractor fees and materials, for $7,000 to $9,000, depending on where you live. The main question—in terms of cost—is where you'll locate the new toilet. If the new fixture cannot be easily plumbed into the existing vent stack, the resulting complications can add thousands of dollars to your remodeling cost. Laundry areas are considered good candidates for conversions because they're already equipped with plumbing. For an attic or basement conversion, it's most economical if you can stack a new bathroom directly over or under an existing one. Attic conversions may require adding or changing roof trusses or beefing up the roof framing.

MAKE A TRADE

Any underused room can be a candidate for gaining the space needed for a new bath. The bath shown here was previously the kitchen of an upstairs apartment. This project is filled with function and character blending today's conveniences with old-fashioned details such as square pillars and wide moldings. An underused spare bedroom is another excellent candidate for conversion to a new bath. Also consider combining two small bedrooms into one luxurious master suite.

OPPOSITE: Natural light and Mission-style lantern fixtures keep the bath warm and bright. The custom vanity combines a three-drawer unit with a made-to-fit cabinet. The same ceramic tile is used on the countertop and floor.

BELOW: The architectural interest of an upstairs kitchen made the ideal spot for a new bathroom.

LEFT: A vaulted ceiling, display niche, and light fixture carry the bath's design themes to the tub-shower area. The door at left leads to a small balcony.

RIGHT: Carve out storage opportunities throughout the bath. This recessed storage niche contains shallow shelves for bottles and a fold-down ironing board.

When working within an existing space, work with what the space has to offer. Here, a custom vanity provides everyday storage and space. A clever built-in unit near the room's entry stores bath and dressing necessities. The room's design mixes in the modern luxury of a whirlpool tub without souring the overall Craftsman flavor.

Add spaciousness, when possible, with a vaulted ceiling. Paneling, moldings, wainscoting and cabinetry of similar colors help create harmony within the room. Work for a balanced combination of light, openness, and charm.

The ultimate compliment for any bathroom is that if it were to lack plumbing fixtures, you would still want to relax there. Keep this goal in mind as you plan your conversion.

Designer Tip

If the area you have in mind for a potential bathroom is short on space, add built-ins to the wall. The built-in unit near this bath's entry adds utility and visual interest without taking up floor space. The arch at the top parallels the shape of the facing doorway.

Showerhead Placement. If a low ceiling prevents you from putting the showerhead as high on the wall as you would like it, install an overhead shower fixture instead. Overhead fixtures also reduce wall splashes, so you may not need a shower door, curtain, or even shower walls. Or install a handheld unit if you want to avoid getting your hair wet each time you shower.

add new space

Adding a bath onto the exterior of your house is generally more expensive than finding room for one inside, but if you don't have space to spare, an addition may be the only choice. In the bath featured here, nostalgic looks complement 21st-century convenience. The new space is built over an existing laundry room and blends with the character of this 1880s Victorian home.

Planning is critical for an addition, particularly for maximizing space. The shower and toilet in this bathroom are tucked against the side wall, where the roof slope begins at 4½ feet, reserving the full-height wall for the cabinetry.

Adding space to an already-existing bathroom will save time and money, compared to building an entirely new addition. Plumbing is expensive, so to keep costs down, leave as many fixtures as you can in their existing locations.

Standard-size vanities and cabinetry are sized for standard-size bathrooms. Uniquely shaped spaces may require custom-built cabinets or shower enclosures to maximize the room's useable space. The white-painted twin medicine cabinets and arched display space above the double vanity in this bathroom are custom-made.

Lighting should also be a top priority. The clear-glass shower stall shown here maximizes light from a high window.

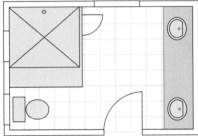

OPPOSITE: You don't need to sacrifice charm for convenience. Detailed cabinetry and chrome accessories add charm, while solid-surface countertops and a double-sink vanity offer modern convenience. Display space between medicine cabinets provides the perfect niche for an antique hair-comb collection.

LEFT: Add a touch of privacy, as shown here with a clever L-shape, beaded-board half-wall. This simple touch provides space for a towel bar and lends privacy to the shower and adjacent toilet in this master bath.

Maximize Comfort.
Look for ways to add on without disrupting the traffic flow in other rooms. Make the new space match the old as closely as possible. New bath windows, for example, should be the same as others in the house. Even if glass block is used only in the new bath space, the size and shape of the glass block window should be consistent with other windows in the home.

• Ventilate. Proper ventilation keeps your bath free of mildew and moisture damage. Install overhead fans and operable windows to let air in and moisture out. Choose a ventilating fan that exchanges all the air in the room eight times or more per hour.

• Add convenience. Allow at least 24 inches of towel-bar space for each person. Plan a towel bar no farther than 6 inches from the tub or shower entrance. Find room for a seat that enables you to towel off and dress comfortably.

• Plan door swings. Consider the direction of shower door and cabinet door swings. Improper planning can create everyday hassles.

• Take design cues from those already established throughout the existing house.

• Trade off openness and privacy as necessary to keep your new bath feeling comfortable, but not crowded. Conserve floor space by replacing swinging doors with pocket ones. Use wall-hung cabinets and freestanding furniture pieces to increase storage.

• If an addition is too costly, a bump-out may be an affordable alternative. A bump-out, a simple extension that can be cantilevered, is less expensive because it does not require its own foundation.

• Whether it's all new or a mix of new and old, your new bathroom can be a timeless addition to your home.

GAIN THROUGH EXPANSION

To gain more square footage than a small bump-out can provide, look for ways to add on without disrupting the traffic flow in other rooms. This bath was expanded with a window-rich addition at the back of the house to transform a bath from dated and dark to voluminous and bright. Because the original bath was located at the back of the house, it was an ideal candidate for an addition. The addition included a 19-foot-wide expansion coupled with the annexation of two small closets. Eliminating one of the closets allowed the door to the bathroom to be moved for better traffic flow. Expanding the bath provided room for a walk-in closet to be positioned within the bath area. The more spacious floor plan also allowed room for a large walk-in shower and whirlpool tub to replace the former tub-shower combination unit.

Several factors impact an addition. Local building codes will determine the building restrictions that apply to your home and property. Knowing what you are able to do early in the process will allow you to focus your plans on a viable option. Involving design professionals early in the planning stages will help you develop solutions that are less disruptive to current traffic patterns, and that better blend with the architecture of your existing home.

OPPOSITE: **Stacking transoms on top of casements emphasizes the height of and allows light to flood this bath addition.**

ABOVE: **Without a door, access to the shower is easy. Clean-up is simple too.**

RIGHT: **One of two matching vanities, this is topped with easy-care solid-surfacing. If space allows, consider including two separate vanities in a large bath such as this one.**

5 outfit your space

Choose materials and fixtures wisely so that your new bath will look great and perform beautifully. »

>> Material choices, such as flooring, countertops, and wall coverings, affect the look, the function, and the cost of your bathroom remodeling. The essential components include sinks, tubs, showers, and toilets. They need to be durable, as well as practical and attractive. Your top priority when choosing these bath components should be how the materials will function given how you, your family, and your guests will use the bathroom.

floors

RIGHT: **A mosaic of broken limestone tiles rings the matte-finish, honed** *crema marfil* **marble floor with rustic texture.**

OPPOSITE: **Hefty 18×18-inch limestone squares punctuated with tiny glass tiles create a spalike feel in the bath.**

Bath and kitchen floors are probably the hardest working surfaces in your home. They must withstand plenty of abuse: overflowing sinks and bathtubs, wet feet, heavy foot traffic, and garden dirt, to name a few. To determine what flooring will work best for you, consider three major criteria: what you need in terms of wear and tear, how the floor will fit into your design, and whether your selection will fit into your budget.

Your best dollar payback will come from equipping your bath with materials, fixtures, and features that have become the standard in comparably priced homes. If you're planning to live in the house for years and resale is less of an issue, make material choices that are as personal as you please.

LAMINATE

While laminate has been used for countertops for decades, it has only been available as a flooring material for a few years. Slightly less expensive than its authentic counterparts, laminate flooring is known for its durability and ease of cleanup, but it does have a slightly hollow feel underfoot. It can be installed over existing flooring. Not all laminates are suitable for installation in moisture-prone rooms, so be sure to check the

manufacturer's warranty before purchasing. Unfortunately, it cannot be refinished if damaged.

Laminate flooring is made from a complex layering process that includes a clear, extremely durable, aluminum oxide top coat; a second layer of plastic resin embedded into a decorative photographic image; a rigid back core, such as medium- or high-density fiberboard; and a backing material designed to prevent warping. Because the decorative image printed on the second layer is a photograph, laminate floors truly look like the wood, stone, or ceramic tile they were designed to impersonate. Laminate comes in three shapes—planks, squares, and rectangles. Oak is the hottest seller, followed by maple. Ceramic tile and natural stone look-alikes are also available. Prices range from $18 to $45 per square yard; add $27 to $36 per square yard for professional installation.

CERAMIC TILE

Clay-base ceramic tiles provide the ideal choice for moisture-prone areas. Floor tiles are extremely durable; are water,

ABOVE: Ash floors paired with a mahogany tub enclosure add a warm, rich look to this bath.

RIGHT: Colorful throw rugs rather than wall-to-wall carpet are ideal for bathrooms. These bright runners connect with the color scheme elsewhere in the bath, provide soft, warm footing on cool mornings, and can be machine washed or dry-cleaned as needed.

LEFT: The dyed concrete floor in this bath offers the durability of ceramic tile without the grout lines. The expansion joints where the two poured slabs meet was a structural necessity, yet its sinuous curve plays up the bath's contemporary design.

BELOW: This floor tile look like limestone, but it is porcelain with mosaiclike insets.

stain, and wear resistant; and are easy to care for. They come in an array of colors, patterns, shapes, and sizes. Tiles 12 inches square or larger are currently the most popular choice. Although tile can feel cold underfoot, it can be warmed with radiant heat coils. For safety purposes, always choose a bath tile that has a slip-resistant finish. Seal all tile grout; otherwise, it can be difficult to clean. Broken tiles cannot be repaired, but they can be replaced.

Ceramic tile costs range from less than $9 per square yard for mass-produced tiles to hundreds of dollars per square yard for commissioned art tiles. To prevent chipping and cracking, install tile only over a firmly supported sub-flooring. Uncomplicated installations costs start at about $9 per square yard and top out at $45 or more per yard for more complicated installations.

STONE TILE

Stone tiles are similar to those used in building construction centuries ago. These tiles are made by slicing boulders and slabs of natural rock into thin squares or rectangles. Not all stone is suitable for use as bath flooring, however. Glossy surfaces require regular polishing and can be slippery when wet. Marble tiles must be sealed to prevent staining and pitting. (Splashed urine will damage marble.) Limestone and slate tiles are also porous; they too must be sealed to prevent dirt and stain absorption. Granite tiles require little or no maintenance; they are nonporous, easy

to clean, and virtually indestructible. For better traction, choose a honed finish.

Like its ceramic counterpart, stone tile needs an extremely stable subsurface that does not give. Stone tile prices vary by region, depending on how far the stone must be shipped. Installation prices range from $9 to $45 per square yard.

CONCRETE

Able to withstand the rigors of heavy traffic, concrete is becoming a popular surface for much-used areas of the home. Easy to clean and versatile, concrete can mimic the look of stone, at a lower cost.

Concrete can be dyed virtually any color, and before it is fully cured it can be stamped to create any sort of surface texture or appearance. Because concrete is very porous, it must be sealed for protection against embedded dirt and stains. Concrete flooring ranges from $36 to

$90 per square yard, installed. (Stamping and etching drive up the cost.)

HARDWOOD

The most familiar type of hardwood flooring is composed of solid, one-piece boards. But there is also a variety called engineered wood flooring that consists of two or more layers of wood laminated together—similar to plywood. The top layers consist of a hardwood veneer; the bottom layers are typically made from softer woods. Due to the limited thickness of the top layer, these engineered woods can be refinished a limited number of times, but they are generally considered more stable for moisture-filled bath installations. Both engineered and solid woods are wear resistant, and they provide a naturally warm look. Because the floor is not as hard as ceramic or stone, it is more comfortable.

All hardwood, whether it is solid or engineered, is vulnerable to moisture. Today's polyurethane finishes stand up to limited amounts of water. You'll want to avoid using hardwood in children's baths or in any bath where excess water is unavoidable. Engineered wood and solid wood floor prices are similar; the cost ranges from $27 to $45 per square yard. Installation prices range from $18 to $45 per square yard.

RESILIENT

All synthetic, resin-based floor coverings come under the resilient flooring category. Resilient flooring includes vinyl tiles and sheet flooring. Sheets up to 15 feet wide eliminate seams in most bathrooms. Once-popular linoleum has fallen out of favor, but it is making a comeback as it is considered an eco-friendly choice.

Resilient flooring is an excellent choice if you have young children. It's flexible, water and stain resistant, and easy to maintain. Because the flooring is relatively soft, it helps muffle noise and is easy on the feet and legs. The softness of the flooring, however, makes it susceptible to denting. Most warranties last no longer than 10 years. Inlaid patterns wear better than patterns applied photographically, as the inlaid image runs throughout the thickness of the material. Vinyl prices range from $9 to $38 per square yard; add a dollar per square yard for installation. Linoleum runs from $40 to $90 per square yard; add $2 per square yard for installation.

CARPET

Slip resistant, warm, and comfortable, carpet muffles sounds. But because it absorbs water, stains easily, and promotes mildew growth, it is usually not recommended for bath installations, particularly in areas adjacent to the toilet, tub, or shower. If you like the feel of carpet underfoot, use washable rugs or have a washable or dry-cleanable carpet runner custom-made to cover the

floor area near the vanity.

Carpet is typically made from one of four fibers: nylon, olefin, polyester, or wool. Wool is the most expensive and most durable (although is it not washable), followed by nylon, polypropylene (also referred to as olefin), and polyester. Nylon and other synthetics are washable. Loop piles will perform better than cut piles over the long haul because the

loops help evenly distribute the impact of foot traffic.

Carpet prices range from a few dollars a square yard for polyester to upwards of $90 per square yard for the finest wool. Decent-quality nylon carpets range from $15 to $30 per square yard. Cushion prices vary from $2.50 to $6 per square yard. Installation costs start at $2 per square yard and go upward.

flooring options

LAMINATE. Pros: Durable. Can be installed over existing floor. Easy to clean and maintain. Wide range of colors and designs imitate wood, stone, or ceramic tile. **Cons:** Cannot be refinished if damaged. Floor can be noisy unless foam underlayment is used. **Cost:** $18–$45 per square yard.

CERAMIC TILE. Pros: Durable. Water and stain resistant. Wide choice of colors, designs, textures, and shapes. Tiles can be mixed for border treatments and field accents. **Cons:** Can be cold and noisy. Glazed tiles can be slippery when wet. Hard on feet. Moisture and dirt can get into grout joints and tiles can stain unless they're sealed. **Cost:** $9 and up per square yard.

STONE TILE. Pros: Virtually indestructible. Easy to maintain. Elegant. Withstands high temperatures. **Cons:** Marble is cold and slippery. Hard on feet. Expensive. Strong subfloor needed. Must be sealed. Limestone and granite readily absorb stains and dirt. Difficult to repair. Gloss surfaces require regular polishing which is costly and messy. **Cost:** Varies by region, depending on how far the stone must be shipped.

CONCRETE. Pros: Hard wearing. Long lasting. Easy to clean. Versatile. Colorful. **Cons:** Prone to staining and cracking. Can feel cold and hard on feet. Requires regular sealing. **Cost:** $36–$90 per square yard installed. Stamping and etching extra.

HARDWOOD. Pros: Wear resistant. Lasts indefinitely. Provides a natural, warm look. Comfortable. Surface finish easy to keep clean. Can be refinished. **Cons:** Vulnerable to moisture. Some woods such as pine dent easily. May darken with age. Waxed surfaces can't be mopped. Some finishes wear unevenly. Some finishes are difficult to repair. **Cost:** $27–$45 per square yard.

RESILIENT. Pros: Comfortable. Water and stain resistant. Easy to install. Simple to clean. Large number of designs. Tiles can be mixed to create custom patterns or color accents. Sheets up to 12 feet wide eliminate seams in smaller rooms. **Cons:** Soft. Prone to dent and tear. Moisture can get into seams between tiles. Doesn't wear as well as other flooring. **Cost:** $9–$90 per square yard.

CARPET. Pros: Slip resistant. Warm and comfortable. Muffles sound. Wide range of colors and styles. Used primarily in dry climates, such as the Southwest. **Cons:** Absorbs water. Stains easily. Promotes mildew growth. Not easy to clean. **Cost:** $3–$90 per square yard.

countertops

When you're ready to select a counter-top material for your bath, look for a material that will suit the style of your bath and that will stand up to water, soap, toothpaste, cosmetics, and acetone- and alcohol-based liquids. You have a large number of styles and materials from which to select.

CERAMIC TILE

As they do for walls and floors, clay-base ceramic tiles make an attractive, durable finish for countertops, especially in moisture-prone areas. The surface tiles are durable, water, stain, and wear resistant; and easy to care for. Heat from rollers or curling irons won't cause damage. They are available in an array of colors, patterns, shapes, and sizes. As with tile flooring, tile grout, if left unsealed, can encourage mildew growth and be difficult to clean.

CONCRETE

Concrete, although it always has a rough-hewn quality, can be colored, scored, and textured to create many interesting looks. In addition, decorative tiles and metals can be inlaid for a custom look. Sinks can be integrated into the countertop. Because concrete is very porous, however, it must be sealed for protection against embedded dirt and stains.

STONE TILES AND SLABS

Stone countertops are extremely durable; granite resists stains and stands up well to water. Slabs are more expensive than tile, but eliminate grouting and grout care. Marble veining, although attractive, makes the marble weaker. Because both marble and limestone are porous stones, they will stain. Proper sealing helps, but doesn't completely eliminate the problem. Granite is less porous and less likely to stain.

Cultured marble resembles solid surfacing but is somewhat less expensive. It is made from natural marble embedded in plastic and requires the same care as plastic laminate countertops. Cultured marble is available in sheet form in standard counter dimensions of 19 and 21 inches deep. As with solid surfacing, sinks can be integrated into the countertop. Once scratched, however, cultured marble cannot be repaired.

OPPOSITE: **Only the edge of this solid-surface countertop is deep. The rest of the solid-surfacing vanity top is just 1/2-inch thick.**

LEFT: **Using mosaic tile for the counter-tops enabled the installers to "roll" the mesh sheets over the countertop edge. In a custom installation such as this one, you can select the colors and tiles for the mosaic, which is then assembled by hand onto mesh sheets prior to installation.**

countertop options

CERAMIC TILE. Pros: Durable. Water and stain resistant. Wide choice of colors, designs, textures, and shapes. (Tiles can be mixed for border treatments and field accents.) Cons: Moisture and dirt can get into grout joints. Tiles can stain unless they're sealed. Very hard; if you drop fragile items on the counter, they will most likely break. Difficult, but possible, to repair. Cost: $18–$90 per linear foot installed.

CONCRETE. Pros: Hard wearing. Long lasting. Easy to clean. Versatile. Colorful. Cons: Prone to staining. Prone to cracking. Requires regular sealing treatments. Cost: $70–$150 per linear foot installed; stamping and etching increase the cost.

HARDWOOD. Pros: Wear resistant. Lasts indefinitely. Provides a warm look. Surface finish easy to keep clean. Can be refinished. Cons: Vulnerable to moisture. Some woods such as pine may dent easily. May darken with age. Some finishes wear unevenly and are difficult to repair. Cost: $40–$75 per linear foot installed.

LAMINATE. Pros: Durable. Inexpensive. Easy to clean and maintain. Wide range of colors and designs can imitate wood, stone, or ceramic tile. Cons: Although durable, it does scratch and it cannot be refinished if damaged. Cost: $26–$60 per running foot installed.

SOLID SURFACING. Pros: Require little maintenance. More durable than laminate. Can repair scratches, abrasions, and minor burns with fine-grade sandpaper. Available in many colors and styles. Sinks can be integrated directly into the countertop. Cons: Intense heat and heavy falling objects can cause damage. Cost: $100–$250 per linear foot installed.

STONE SLAB. Pros: Virtually indestructible. Easy to maintain, especially granite. Elegant. Withstands high temperatures. Cons: Expensive. Marble and limestone readily absorb stains and dirt. Difficult to repair. Gloss surfaces require regular polishing, which is costly and messy. Cost: Vary by region, depending on how far the stone must be shipped; for most areas of the country estimate $125–$250 per running foot installed.

SOLID SURFACING

Cast from an acrylic resin, solid-surface countertops require little maintenance and are more durable than laminate. Intense heat and heavy falling objects can cause damage, but scratches, abrasions, and minor burns can be repaired with fine-grade sandpaper. Solid-surface countertops are available in more colors and styles than ever before. Edge treatments range from a simple, smooth edge that imitates stone to intricate inlaid designs in contrasting colors. Sinks can be integrated directly into the countertop—no seams to clean.

BELOW: **Solid-surface countertops are easy to keep clean.**

WOOD

Wood counters are attractive, versatile, and easy to install, but they are especially vulnerable to water damage. Their porosity makes them difficult to keep sanitary. Whatever type of wood you choose, you must seal it with a marine-quality polyurethane varnish to make it a viable selection for the bath. Special care should be taken to seal around the edges of plumbing fixtures so standing water can't seep in and cause warping or wood rot.

ABOVE AND LEFT: A 2-inch solid-maple countertop matches the vanity. The countertop was custom-stained nutmeg brown and then sealed with a clear catalyzed-conversion varnish for moisture resistance.

LAMINATE

Affordably priced, laminate is still the most widely used countertop surfacing material. Similar in construction to laminate floors, these countertops are made from layers of plastic sheeting and particleboard bonded together under heat and pressure. Laminate countertops clean easily and are resistant to water and stains. They do scratch, can wear thin, and dull over time. Hard blows can chip or dent the plastic; a damaged counter cannot be repaired.

Available in multiple patterns and colors, textures range from smooth and glossy to a mottled, leatherlike look. Stone-look finishes are currently most popular.

Fabricated laminated countertops come in two forms: prefab or special order. Fabricated counters are made from bonding laminate sheeting over a ¾-inch-thick particleboard core. Exposed edges can be adorned with matching laminate or with a contrasting decorative edging. Installing the finished countertop is not difficult, although larger pieces can be somewhat bulky and difficult to handle. It is also possible to buy sheets of laminate material and attach it to a particleboard counter yourself, but this takes special tools and can be somewhat time consuming. A professional will likely do the best job.

BELOW: **Mosaic ceramic tile creates a colorful countertop in this bath. White grout and tiles require frequent cleaning and maintenance to remain looking their best.**

ABOVE: Seemingly tinted by time, pitted travertine ascends from countertop to backsplash to a display shelf, reminiscent of a feature found on old washstands.

LEFT: Granite is less porous and less likely to stain than other natural countertop materials, making it a durable choice. Solid granite is expensive, but a small countertop such as this one can be affordable. Granite tiles are another less expensive option for larger countertops.

Alternative Choices. More materials are being put to work as bath countertops. Slate, soapstone, and other natural stones are gaining in popularity. Similar in price to other natural stones, both slate and soapstone are very durable and require less care than marble.

Stainless steel is another material seeing more bath duty. It's easy to clean and adds sleek texture. Copper, brass, and other metals can also be used but may require additional care and sealing treatments. Check with the metal supplier for specific usage recommendations.

Glass slabs create a dramatic effect and work well in guest baths or in rooms that are not used on a daily basis. Frosted glass hides scratches and water spots better than clear glass.

wallcoverings

Walls are the largest surface in the bath, so how you adorn them makes a significant impact on the feel of the room. Whether you choose paint, tile, paneling, or wallpaper, remember that your covering of choice for the bathroom must stand up to heat, humidity, and frequent cleaning. Mix and match materials to meet your durability requirements and to create a look that is both attractive and practical.

TILE

Ceramic and natural stone tiles are attractive, durable, and easy to clean. Most are stain resistant and—when installed correctly—fully waterproof. Although ceramic wallcoverings are more expensive than other wallcoverings, their longevity makes them worth considering for at least the wettest areas of the bath.

Like floor and countertop tiles, wall tiles come glazed and unglazed, plain and patterned, and in a vast array of colors. Stock tiles can be mixed and matched with custom-painted tiles to create an individual look. Wall tiles are not as durable as floor and countertop tiles because they typically do not have to withstand the same kind of abuse. Because of this, you may use floor and countertop tiles on the walls, but you should not use wall tiles on the countertops or floors.

You can apply ceramic tile to any drywall, plaster, or plywood surface that's smooth, sound, and firm. Unglazed tile should be properly sealed. Slightly less expensive than floor and countertop tile, wall tile prices start at $15 per linear foot, installed, and go up from there.

GLASS BLOCK

Glass block is popular because of its sleek spa look and its ability to transmit light while preserving some amount of privacy. It can be used to create walls, shower surrounds, and windows. Glass block costs range from $45 to $65 per square foot, installed.

ABOVE: You'll probably move or redecorate before you'll need to replace a ceramic tile wall. Because the material is so very durable, it's a great choice for children's or family baths. Be sure to choose a color and pattern that you will continue to like well into the future.

OPPOSITE: A wall of glass block between the steam shower and tub keeps the shower feeling bright and spacious. You can find glass blocks that are somewhat transparent, as well as those that are nearly opaque, and many options between these extremes. Choose the kind of glass block for your bath that best meets your privacy needs.

PAINT

Paint is the least-expensive option and the easiest wallcovering to change whether you tire of it or it starts to look tired. Painting is also an easy do-it-your-self project; the majority of the time involved is spent masking and draping the surfaces you wish to keep paint-free. Combine paint with a latex glaze to create paint treatments that have the look of wallpaper. Tone-on-tone creamy beige-color paints rubbed over with several layers of latex glaze, for example, create a parchment paper look. Most home centers offer painting kits (from $30 to $70 each) that include the instructions and the necessary tools to create a number of painting techniques, such as sponging or rag rolling.

Today's latex water-base paints are as durable as many of their alkyd oil-base counterparts. Unlike their alkyd counterparts, latex paints dry quicker and clean up with soap and water. Look for a paint finish that is washable, scrubbable, and moisture resistant. Paints specified for bathroom use are more expensive but can be worth the investment in terms of durability.

If you want to cover a porcelain, plastic, or tile surface, look for an epoxy paint designated for that specific purpose. Most surfaces must be primed to ensure proper

paint adhesion. Quality paint prices range from $20 to $30 per gallon.

VINYL WALLCOVERINGS

Vinyl wallcoverings (a more durable choice for the bath than wallpapers) come in a vast array of colors, patterns, styles, and textures. Many come with a prepasted adhesive coating that only needs to be dampened to adhere to the wall.

When it comes to the bath, it's best to choose a vinyl covering that is laminated to a fabric backing instead of a covering that is all or partly paper. Vinyl coverings withstand moisture much better than papers do. Products labeled "scrubbable" are the most durable and will tolerate more abrasion than the "washable" ones. Although not recommended for full baths, standard wallpapers can be used in powder rooms or in areas of the bath that are not subjected to splashes or condensation. Wallcovering prices range from $20 to $150 or more per single roll. Coverings from major manufacturers typically run from $25 to $40 per roll.

WOOD PANELING

Wood adds a natural warmth that complements many interior design themes.

Look Up. Keep in mind that you'll need a proper ceiling finish to complete your bath. Any variation from a standard 8-foot-high white ceiling will make a dramatic impact on the overall look of the room. A 9-, 10-, or 11-foot-high ceiling adds volume to a small space. Painting the ceiling lighter than the walls makes it appear to recede even further. If your bath is especially large and has a high ceiling, you can create a more intimate feel by painting the ceiling a shade or two darker than the walls. Darker shades make a ceiling look lower than its actual height. Another option is to recess the center portion of the ceiling and install cove lighting around the perimeter.

Beaded-board paneling or wooden planks add a warm, rustic look to a room. Covering the ceiling with a faux-painted treatment or a subtly patterned wallcovering draws the eye upward. For an old-fashioned look, use the same vintage print wallcovering on both the ceiling and the walls. As with darker shades of paint, if the treatment or pattern you select is dark or bold, the ceiling will seem lower. Don't pick a paper that's too busy or the printed ceiling will overwhelm the room.

As a wall-surfacing material, it comes in the form of premilled solid wainscoting or tongue-and-groove beaded board, veneered plywood, or melamine-surfaced hardboard. Both solid wood and plywood-backed veneers must be sealed with a water-resistant coating, such as polyurethane. Hardboard panels coated with melamine (a thin layer of white plastic) are well-suited for baths because melamine is water resistant and easy to clean.

LEFT: A woven wall covering in warm chocolate brown with bronze threads lends rich texture to this powder room where moisture is not a factor. Read the manufacturer's usage recommendations before applying any wallcovering to a full bath. Vinyl wallcoverings offer a good choice for bath walls because they are not easily damaged by moisture and they can be wiped clean with a damp cloth.

RIGHT: Wooden wainscoting creates vintage charm. Proper preparation and painting helps to seal the wood from the potential damage of a steamy bathroom.

BELOW LEFT AND RIGHT: Subway-style tile lends vintage charm to this bath. Glass tiles are used as an accent.

sinks

Bathroom sinks come in more sizes, shapes, and material choices than ever before. You can purchase round, oval, rectangular, or asymmetrical bowls. Each shape is available in several color choices, although white still outsells all the other colors combined. Some of the more expensive models are adorned with hand-painted designs. Or you can indulge in having a standard sink custom-painted to match your decor.

Before you choose the right one (or two) for your bath, consider how often the sink will be used. Sinks used in powder rooms and guest baths typically receive less use, so durability and maintenance are lesser issues in these spaces than in master baths and children's baths.

In frequently used baths, choose materials to match the kind of wear and tear your family will instigate. Choose larger, deeper sinks to reduce splashing and countertop cleanup. To ensure a good match in terms of design, consider purchasing a matching sink, toilet, and bathtub.

sink options

VESSEL SINKS. Installation: Most rest in a custom-cut hole in the vanity top. Details: Make a dramatic design statement. Appear to sit atop the vanity counter. Cost: $300–$700 for most models.

INTEGRAL SINKS. Installation: Part of the same material as the vanity counter. Details: Easy to clean because there is no joint between the bowl and the countertop. If either the sink or counter is damaged beyond repair, the entire unit must be replaced. Cost: $200–$500.

SELF-RIMMING OR SURFACE-MOUNT SINKS. Installation: Top edge rests on top of the counter after the sink is dropped into a hole large enough to accommodate the sink bowl. Rim forms a tight seal with the countertop to prevent leaks. Details: Easiest to install because the hole need not be a perfect cut as it is hidden below the rim once the sink is in place. Cost: Basic drop-in sinks start at $75.

UNDERMOUNT SINKS. Installation: Attached to the bottom of the countertop; require an exact cut for installation. Details: Clean tailored look. Can be somewhat difficult to clean underneath the lip where the sink and counter seals together. Cost: Start at $75.

RIMMED SINKS. Installation: Sit slightly above the countertop with a tight-fitting metal rim joining the sink and the countertop. Require a nearly perfect cut for installation. Details: The rim is made of different finishes to match whatever type of faucet you select. Cost: Start at $70.

STYLES

Sinks fall into three main categories:

Pedestal. These sinks fit on top of a pedestal-shape base and are an ideal solution for a small bath. The disadvantage of a pedestal sink is that it offers little counterspace and no base cabinet storage below. Simple pedestals start at $125.

Wall hung. Like pedestal sinks, wall-hung styles have the advantage of squeezing into small spaces. They have the same disadvantages of pedestal sinks with one more—there is no pedestal to hide any plumbing lines. To make up for this, some sinks have brass legs to offer a more finished look underneath. Wall-hung sinks are often the preferred choice in universally designed baths because

OPPOSITE: A stainless-steel-and-glass pedestal sink serves as a dramatic focal point in this small bathroom. Because this style offers no storage space below, plan for other storage options such as the towel rack above the toilet and the wall-mounted soap holder. The glass surround offers limited space for supplies while grooming.

LEFT: Undermounted below a green granite countertop, this sink requires a perfect cut in the stone. The smooth countertop makes it easy to wipe spills directly into the sink.

they can be installed at any height and have a clear space underneath that allows for seated knee space and wheelchair access. These sinks start at $80.

Vanity sinks. Vanity sinks have lots of countertop space around them as well as cabinet storage below. Vanity sinks, however, require the most floor space of any sink style. Vanity sinks can be installed in several ways, depending on the type of sink you select. See "Sink Options" on page 99.

ABOVE: A self-rimming sink is easy to install because the hole does not have to be perfectly cut. Careful cleaning is required to keep the seam between the sink and counter free of dirt.

ABOVE RIGHT: Vessel sinks sit on top of the counter like a bowl. Most require wall-mount faucets and a specialized drainpipe fitting.

OPPOSITE: A custom console vanity supports this shapely sink in an Asian-influenced bathroom. Similar sinks can be purchased as part of a console-vanity unit.

material choices

PORCELAIN-ENAMELED CAST IRON. Pros: **Extremely durable. Easy to care for.** Considerations: **Somewhat heavy. Requires a sturdy support system.**

VITREOUS CHINA. Pros: **Lustrous surface. Not as heavy as porcelain-enameled cast-iron sinks. Most resistant to discoloration and corrosion.** Considerations: **Can be chipped or cracked when struck by a heavy object.**

SOLID SURFACE. Pros: **May be integrated directly into the countertop. Fine-grade sandpaper will remove shallow nicks and scratches.** Considerations: **These offer varying degrees of durability based on the material from which they are made. Sinks made from the same acrylic resin as quality solid-surface countertops are the most durable and require little maintenance. Polyester and cultured marble sinks share similar properties but scratch and dull more readily.**

STAINLESS STEEL. Pros: **Durable. Unaffected by household chemicals.** Considerations: **Tends to show hardwater and soap spots.**

GLASS. Pros: **Smooth finish is easy to clean. Frosted glass shows water spotting less than its clear counterpart.** Considerations: **Requires extra care to prevent scratching or breaking. Shows water spotting.**

faucets

As you shop for faucets, you'll see everything from traditional, two-handled models that look much like they did a century ago, to the newest one-handle designs that look like contemporary sculpture. Don't make a selection based on looks alone; durability is the key to your continued satisfaction. Comfort in your hand as you turn water on and off is also a factor given how many times you'll use the faucet. You'll also need to make sure that the faucet set you select is the proper size and design to fit your sink. Most vanity sinks come with holes drilled in their rims to accommodate standard faucets and plumbing. These three basic faucet styles are designed to fit the predrilled holes:

Single-handle faucets. These faucets have one spout and one handle, as the one shown *opposite*, that controls the flow of both hot and cold water.

Center-set faucets. With a spout and handle(s) in one unit, these faucets may have either single-handle or double-handle controls. Most are designed for a three-hole basin, with the outside holes spaced 4 inches from center to center. However, some have a single-post design that requires only one hold.

Spread-fit faucets. These faucets separate spout and handles. The connection between them is concealed below

One Handle or Two?
Both popular design choices, one-handle designs are easier to use than their two-handle counterparts. With a little practice on a one-handle model, you can find the temperature you want on the first try. You can also turn the water on with your elbow or wrist when your hands are full or dirty.

Two-handle faucets, on the other hand, offer a more traditional look and you can combine different handles and spouts for a custom look.

the sink deck. They can be adapted to fit holes spaced from 4 to 10 inches apart. They can be individualized even more if they are mounted on a countertop next to the sink. For example, the spout can be placed on a rear corner and the handles off to one side. These faucets are handy for tight installations where there is not enough room for a full faucet at the back of the sink basin. They are also ideal for whirlpool tubs, so that the handles are accessible from outside the tub for filling.

Wall-mount faucets. A fourth faucet type is attached to the wall as opposed to the sink or the counter, as shown above the vessel sink on page 100. These faucets were designed for unusually shaped sinks, such as old-fashioned farm sinks, antique bowls, or other vessels that have been modified for use in the bath.

WHAT'S INSIDE COUNTS

Faucet prices start at $60 for the most basic models and can run as high as $1,000 or more for a waterfall tub faucet. Solid-brass, die-cast innards are a sign of quality, but often come with a hefty price tag—anywhere from $300 to $600 or more. Beware of faucets with plastic shells or handles. Although appealing in price, their durability may be lacking.

Faucet mechanisms have come a long way beyond the simple valve stem with replaceable washers that wore out every few years (although this type of faucet is still on the market today). Precision metal parts, synthetic materials, and hard ceramics have made the washerless faucet commonplace, and on those rare occasions when maintenance is required, the repair is a simple matter of replacing a modular assembly. Ceramic disk faucets can go from off to a full torrent in only a quarter turn of the handle.

finish options

CHROME (polished, brushed, or matte). Pros: **Extremely hard. Easily cleaned. Doesn't oxidize. Matte chrome has a softer appearance and is as durable as polished chrome.** Cons: **Inexpensive chrome sprayed over plastic parts tends to peel.**

BRASS (polished, satin finish, or antique finish). Pros: **Titanium finishes resist scratching, fading, and corrosion.** Cons: **Standard brass finishes are prone to scratching, tarnishing, and corrosion.**

BAKED-ON ENAMEL OR EPOXY COATINGS (available in many colors). Pros: **Wide choice of colors. Easy to clean.** Cons: **May chip or fade; some chemicals may damage color.**

GOLD PLATE (polished, brushed, or matte). Pros: **Visual appeal. Quality gold won't tarnish. Matte finishes hide scratches.** Cons: **Expensive. Quality varies. Finish must be sealed by manufacturer or the gold can be damaged.**

OTHER METALS (polished, brushed, or matte). Pros: **Metals such as nickel offer visual appeal and durability.** Cons: **Can be expensive. Quality varies by the manufacturer.**

OPPOSITE: **Spread-fit faucets provide some design flexibility in that you can choose (within 10 inches) just how much space you want between the handles and the spout. This chrome gooseneck faucet offers greater clearance for washing.**

ABOVE: **Single-handle faucets are convenient because you control both the water temperature and the strength of the water flow with one hand. But note how close the spigot is to the edge of the bowl—this could make handwashing difficult.**

showerheads

More showers are being equipped with a combination of showerheads as opposed to a single wall-mount unit. All shower-heads are rated according to flow rate, or the number of gallons of water they spray per minute (gpm). Water-consuming showerheads deliver as many as 8 gpms. Low-flow models use just 2.5 gpms and today's low-flow models do just as good a job of cleaning as their water-consuming counterparts. Your home's water pressure is also a factor. Either showerhead type can be adjusted for a spray that varies from fine to coarse, and a water action that ranges from a gentle pulsation to a vigorous massage.

The following types of spray heads are available:

Standard wall-mount showerhead. These heads are the most economical and can be adjusted slightly by moving the shower neck. Models that offer vary-ing spray types fit the needs of most users.

Top-mount showerhead. These showerheads work well in areas where the ceiling is too low to accommodate a wall-mount head. Because the spray comes from overhead, it is difficult to avoid getting your hair wet when bathing in this type of shower.

Handheld showerhead. These clip-held showerheads are attached to a 3- to 6-foot-long gooseneck hose that enables you to move the spray of water where you want it. The gooseneck hose adds versatility when it comes to wash-ing your hair or rinsing off. And when it comes time to scrub down the shower enclosure, handheld sprays also get the job done more efficiently. A handheld showerhead also provides for a quick rinse-off after a tub bath.

Sliding bar showerhead. These showerheads, *opposite below,* slide up and down on a bar mounted on the wall. Because the height of the spray is easy to adjust, it's a good option when there is a

Plumbing Layouts. When placing fixtures in your bathroom, think about how they are used and in what order. The sink, for example, should be positioned clos-est to the door because it's often the only fixture used or the last stop in most people's bathing routines. The tub and shower can be farthest from the door because they are not used as frequently.

How you lay out your fixtures can also affect your plumbing bill. The fewer "wet walls" you have, the less costly your plumbing bill will be. One-wall layouts, with fix-tures arranged along a single wall, are the simplest and require the fewest plumbing fittings. If you are unhappy with the functionality of a one wet-wall bath, the money you save may cost you another remodeling in the future.

One-Wall Layout. A design with all the supply and draining pipes located within one wall is more cost efficient but limits your design possibilities. You may want to consider this layout if you are creating an entirely new bath space and have to supply water to the area.

Two-Wall Layout. A design with plumbing in two walls requires more plumbing work but offers more floor area and storage space around the sink.

Three-Wall Layout. Three-wall layouts offer the most design flexibility, but they require more space and more complex plumbing systems.

significant variation in the heights of the people using the shower.

Body spray and body mist shower sprays. These heads or sprays are installed in vertical rows on opposite or adjacent walls, creating a crisscross water massage between the knee and shoulder levels that allows users to quickly wash without getting their hair wet.

Body spa shower panels. These panels are installed against one or more walls of the shower stall and are quipped with water jets arranged vertically from knee to neck level. Similar to jets in a whirlpool tub, the water jets pump out and recirculate large quantities of water for a powerful massage.

Most showerhead/faucet handle combinations cost from $75 for a standard model to $1,500 plus for a panel that includes multiple sprays and a handheld showerhead.

TOP RIGHT: **An English-style faucet offers a stationary spout and a convenient handle-head sprayer.**

RIGHT: **The large, high showerhead lets water flow downward rather than in the face. The sliding bar showerhead to the right is a good choice in a bath where bathers of different heights use the same shower. The head can be easily adjusted to spray higher or lower.**

bathtubs,
whirlpools, and soaking tubs

Most people who want to replace a bathtub are doing it because they either want a larger model or they are stepping up to a deep soaking tub or whirlpool. Before making such an investment, you and your family members should sit in the tub to make sure it fits. Likewise, you'll need to find out if the tub you want will both fit in the space you are allocating for it and will go through your existing doorways. (Getting your old bathtub out of the house may test your ingenuity and your patience.) If the tub you want won't fit through the doors, stairwells, and hallways that connect to your bathroom, your only choice will be to downsize the tub or knock out an exterior wall.

Most bathroom floors can handle 40 pounds of weight per square foot. A large-capacity tub may require extra bracing so that the floor can support it once it is filled with water.

If you're installing a whirlpool, you'll also need to have access to the pump

OPPOSITE: **This whirlpool tub offers eight jets to soothe aching muscles. Platform-style tubs are installed in a fashion similar to a self-rimming sink; the tub simply drops into a separate platform, making installation versatile.**

BELOW: **Intended for relaxing parental soaks, this large claw-foot tub also measures up to children's bathtime splashes. Freestanding claw-foot tubs can be installed virtually anywhere in a room.**

ABOVE: Extending the deck of this marble tub provides a stylish bench in the shower. A step makes it easier to access the tub.

Getting in Hot Water.

The National Kitchen and Bath Association recommends that your hot water heater be at least two-thirds the capacity of your tub: a 60-gallon hot water tank will serve a 90-gallon tub adequately, but the rest of the water in your house will be cold. The tub's manual will tell you how many gallons of water it will take to fill it.

If your hot water heater is too small, you can either install a bigger heater or install two linked heaters side by side. You can also buy a whirlpool tub with an in-line heater of its own. Instead of heating water before use like a hot water tank, an inline heater maintains the temperature of the water for the duration of your bath. If you plan to soak for long periods, an in-line heater is a good idea, regardless of the capacity of your hot water heater.

(typically installed near one end of the tub) in case repairs are necessary. To make your whirlpool bath more soothing, choose a pump that is quiet and offers a wide range of massage options.

Both whirlpool and standard bathtubs come in four basic designs:

Recessed tubs. With one finished side called an apron, a recessed tub fits between two end walls and against a back wall. Models are available with a drain at either end to fit your plumbing needs. People with limited mobility may find it difficult to get in and out of these tubs.

Corner tubs. Space-saving corner tubs fit diagonally between two corners and, like standard apron tubs, have only one finished side. Other corner options are also similar to apron tubs, except the tubs have both a finished side and end with one rounded, finished end.

Freestanding tubs. These tubs are finished on all four sides and can be placed most anywhere in the room. Freestanding claw-foot tubs look appropriate in traditional and vintage baths. You can also find freestanding tubs—such as a pedestal design—that have a more contemporary look.

Platform tubs. These tubs have no finished panels; they are dropped into a platform. Platform tubs can be placed anywhere depending on the platform's design: into a corner, against a long wall, or in the center of the room.

Bathtub prices start at about $150 for a basic 5-foot model and can cost more than $5,000 for a high-end whirlpool.

BELOW: **A pedestal-style soaking tub is the centerpiece of this indulgent master bath.**

Made from Scratch. Can't find anything to fit your needs? Forgo a standard tub for a custom-made stone or tile enclosure with conveniences designed specifically for you. This tub was custom contoured to fit the homeowners' body shapes. The couple sat in a mesh form before the tub was tiled to ensure the proper curvature.

ABOVE AND BELOW: Deep soaking tubs are replacing whirlpools in many baths as the luxury bathing amenity of choice. Steps provide easier access to this tub. A recessed television allows bathers viewing pleasure while relaxing.

material choices

ENAMELED CAST IRON. Details: Constructed from iron molded into a bathtub shape. Finished with enamel. Pros: Thicker than other materials. Retains the heat of the water very well. Durable and solid. Variety of color options. Considerations: Heavy, so you may need to reinforce the flooring below the tub.

ENAMELED STEEL. Details: Produced by spraying enamel onto molded steel and firing the tub at a high temperature. Pros: Less expensive than cast iron. Not as heavy as cast iron. Considerations: Chips more readily. Fewer color options. Can be noisier when being filled with water.

FIBERGLASS. Details: Fiberglass backing material is finished with a layer of polyester. Wood or metal reinforcement is added to make the tub feel solid. Pros: Inexpensive. Wide choice of styles and shapes. Lightweight. Considerations: Polyester finish is not as durable as acrylic. Does not retain heat well.

ACRYLIC. Details: Sheets of acrylic are heated and formed in a mold, then reinforced with fiberglass and a wood or metal backing. Pros: Wide choice of styles and shapes. Holds heat better than fiberglass, if properly insulated. Considerations: More expensive than fiberglass. Finish can scratch.

CAST POLYMER. Details: Solid-color, polymer-base materials are used to create these tubs that are often made to resemble a natural stone, such as granite or marble. Pros: Thicker than acrylic, the tub holds heat well. Considerations: Not as durable as either acrylic or enameled cast-iron tubs.

showers

When space and budget allow, including a separate shower in the bathroom layout is a luxurious choice. Separate fixtures mean two people can bathe at the same time. Shower stalls are also easier to get in and out of and easier to clean than combination tub/shower units. If space and budget are limited, make a combination unit safer by selecting a nonslip bottom and grab bars. There are three basic types of separate shower stalls:

Prefabricated stalls. Available in a wide variety of shapes and colors, these stalls are available in one-piece, two-piece, or three-piece versions. The most common material for these units is fiberglass with a finish surface of acrylic or other plastic. Tempered glass combined with fiberglass stalls is also available. Sizes range from 32 inches square (not large enough to meet some local codes) to 36×48 inches. One-piece versions are typically reserved for new construction and new additions. Like a bathtub or whirlpool, one-piece stalls are very large and can be difficult to get into the room. Two- and three-piece models readily fit within most door openings. Doors (or curtains) are typically sold separately. Some come with their own pan—or flooring piece—while others require a separate pan.

Prefabricated stalls are available in three shapes: square, rectangular, and neoangle. They are designed to fit against a wall or into a corner. Corner or neo-angle models have two finished sides and a diagonal front. Most prefabricated units are made of fiberglass finished with either an acrylic or polyester gel coat. The walls of the stall need to be attached to standard wall framing for support. Prefabricated stalls range in price from $250 (for acrylic) to $1,000 or more for glass.

Prefabricated shower pans. These molded flooring pieces are available in a range of materials from plastic to stone.

They can be combined with prefabricated shower stalls, or custom-made acrylic plastic, solid-surface walls, or tiled shower walls. Prices start at about $75.

Custom-made stalls. These stalls offer the most design flexibility; there's no limit on the size or the style of a custom-made shower. Any waterproof material can be used for the walls, including tile, marble, solid surfacing, tempered glass, or glass blocks. Prices vary, depending on materials used, as well as the size and complexity of the shower stall's design.

OPPOSITE: **Custom glass shower walls reveal an oval tile pattern in the shower stall. To save space, a teak-and-chrome shower seat can be folded up when not in use. A recessed niche stores shower gels and shampoos.**

Steam It Up. Equip your shower stalls with a top and a door that seals tightly and you can use the stall as a steam bath. If you want to do this, you'll need to install a vapor barrier on the ceiling and wall framing to keep the moisture from reaching the studs and joists, which will cause wood rot. You'll also need to have a steam generator installed somewhere outside the shower.

BELOW: Pair a bidet with a toilet for the convenience of both in close proximity. Just leave enough space between the two.

OPPOSITE: A sleek toilet with its tank mounted inside the wall and only the bowl and panellike flush mechanism visible in the room make the most of a small bath.

toilets and bidets

A toilet may be utilitarian, but that doesn't mean it can't be stylish. Design choices range from classic two-piece models to sleek low-profile single-piece wall-mounted models.

Choose a toilet that fits both your comfort level and the look you are trying to create. Whether you are purchasing all new fixtures or just one, make sure the unit you select matches or complements the color and style of the other fixtures in your bath.

Models with elongated bowls are more comfortable and more expensive than standard round toilets. Toilet heights range from the standard 14 inches up to 17 inches high. The taller toilets are more comfortable for tall people or people with disabilities.

THE LOWDOWN ON LOW FLOW

By law, toilets manufactured after January 1, 1994, may use no more than 1.6 gallons of water per flush. Models manufactured before this date use 3.5 or more gallons per flush. Unfortunately, many of the low-flow models introduced in the mid-1990s did not work very well. Because of this, they often have to be flushed twice to get the job done, so they don't save much water. Today's low-flow toilets work much better than those early models.

THE BIDET

Although bidets are not used as widely in the United States as they are in Europe, they are gaining in popularity. The fixture resembles a toilet, but actu-ally works more like a sink. Water ascends from the center of the bowl to rinse off the posterior of the person sitting on the bowl. Both genders can safely use a bidet.

Unlike a toilet, a bidet must be plumbed with both hot and cold water, as well as a drain. For convenience, locate the bidet close to the toilet. If the two fixtures are installed side by side, leave at least 15 inches between them.

Expect the fixture to take up at least 3 square feet of floor space.

If you don't have the space or budget for a separate bidet, bidet seats are an option. These models replace most toilet seats and offer a washing and bidet nozzle. Prices are approximately $500.

Combination toilet and bidet units are available for baths lacking space but not lacking luxury. Prices range from $3,000–$5,000.

low-flow options

GRAVITY-FLUSH. The weight of the water flowing down from the tank clears the bowl. The water pressure in your neighborhood will affect how gravity-assisted toilets work. Most manufacturers recommend about 25 pounds per square inch to work best. (Your water pressure can also fluctuate with household activities, such as turning on the lawn sprinklers.) Pros: Least expensive low-flow option. Relatively easy to install. Cons: Does not discharge waste as effectively as the other options. Cost: Starts near $100.

PRESSURE-ASSISTED. Pressurized air created from a vessel hidden in the toilet tank forces water into the bowl and down the drain. Pros: Most effective low-flow option. Cons: Noisier than gravity flush. More expensive to repair. Cost: One-piece units with a pressure-assisted flush range from $300 to $600.

PUMP-ASSISTED. An electric pump propels water into the bowl and down the drain. Pros: Quieter than pressure-assisted toilets and works nearly as well. Cons: Most expensive. Cost: Starts around $600.

If you want to keep your current toilet, but would like to reduce its water consumption, you can displace some of the water in the tank by placing a water-filled plastic bottle into the tank. Or you can install a dual flusher that allows a half-flush for liquid-only flushes.

cabinetry

Grime-Fighting Cabinets. Cabinets that have flat doors with a baked-on finish are easiest to clean. Stained cabinets with a flat or no-gloss finish don't show as much dirt, but they are more easily marred and harder to touch up. Elaborate cabinetry molding is harder to clean.

Choose cabinet pulls and handles that keep you from getting the cabinet surface dirty instead of doors and drawers that you have to reach under to open. D-shape pulls work nicely; they let you open the door or drawer with one finger. In drawers that contain potentially messy items, such as toothpaste and lipstick tubes, install removable acrylic liners that can be thrown into the dishwasher when they become soiled.

The vanity area often serves as a focal point for your bathroom and helps define the entire design. The modest single-sink vanity cabinet has given way to a host of bathroom cabinetry options, from double-sink vanities to custom storage hutches. Bath cabinets are available in an ever-increasing array of styles, materials, and color choices. As with kitchen cabinets, you can purchase bath cabinets in modular (stock) units or you can have one custom-designed and built by a cabinet shop.

There is no rule against using kitchen cabinets in the bath; the only difference is that vanity cabinets are typically 29 to 30 inches high while kitchen base cabinets are typically 36 inches high. Similarly, vanity cabinets' front-to-back depth is 18 to 21 inches, while the front-to-back depth of kitchen cabinets typically runs 24 inches deep. Many people find the 36-inch height more comfortable for standing. If the people who share the bathroom are of significantly different heights, you may want

OPPOSITE: **A dark nutmeg finish on the contemporary vanity creates a striking contrast to the white marble countertop.**

ABOVE: **Furniture-style doors, drawers, moldings, legs, and hardware set a traditional tone and make this cabinetry attractive enough for the dining room. The mahogany units are adorned with maple accents that resemble bamboo.**

For more storage ideas, see Organization Strategies on pages 142–151.

storage of undergarments and sleepwear. Instead of adding a closet or more built-in cabinets, increase bath storage by including freestanding furniture pieces, such as a chest of drawers, into your bath's design. Maximize each piece's storage capacity by customizing the shelves inside to fit the exact items you plan to store.

BE CREATIVE

Bring a jewelry box into the bath and fill it with cosmetics and hair accessories. Use glass shelves to fill empty wall space behind a tub or toilet. Fill recessed stud space with medicine cabinets or open shelves. Add an open storage and display hutch between two existing sinks. Plan open storage niches for neat, yet handy, storage.

ABOVE: Shirred cotton print fabric adds color, pattern, and texture to white-painted maple cabinetry. The vanity top is at 36 inches—the height considered standard for kitchen countertops—because the homeowners decided it was the most comfortable height.

OPPOSITE: Floor-to-ceiling cabinets and sink vanities flank a cosmetics counter. Toe rails make each piece look like a separate item of furniture.

to customize the height of each vanity (or vanity section).

Most standard, also called stock, vanities run 18 inches front to back. Widths start out at 18 inches and continue in 6-inch increments to 72 inches. Matching filler pieces can be used to adapt a standard vanity to fit most any space. Semicustom cabinets are similar to stock cabinets in that these cabinet lines offer standard styles and finishes, but increased size options, usually within 3-inch increments, are offered. Cabinets designed and built specifically for the bath where they will be used are called custom.

When planning your vanity, allow enough room in the front of the vanity for the doors and drawers to open and close without interference. There should be enough wall space for a mirror and light fixtures. If either side of the vanity is exposed and a corner juts out into the room, consider curved edges to prevent painful bumps from occurring.

Plan for the amount of storage you will need by making a list of the specific items you will store there, from toiletries and grooming supplies to towels, cleaning supplies, and toilet paper.

How the cabinets are made and what the cabinets are made from has direct bearing on the price. Solid wood components are more expensive and more durable than veneered woods glued over fiberboard.

Bath cabinet prices range from approximately $35 to $160 per linear foot, including installation.

STORE MORE

Add convenience to your dressing routine by allocating some bath drawers for

Out of the Box. When planning cabinetry, think a bit unconventionally and use every inch, particularly in a small bath, to create storage possibilities. Mount a wall cabinet above the toilet or on the wall above both sides of a pedestal sink. Combine freestanding pieces with more standard built-in cabinetry to maximize wall and floor space, and to personalize your bathroom.

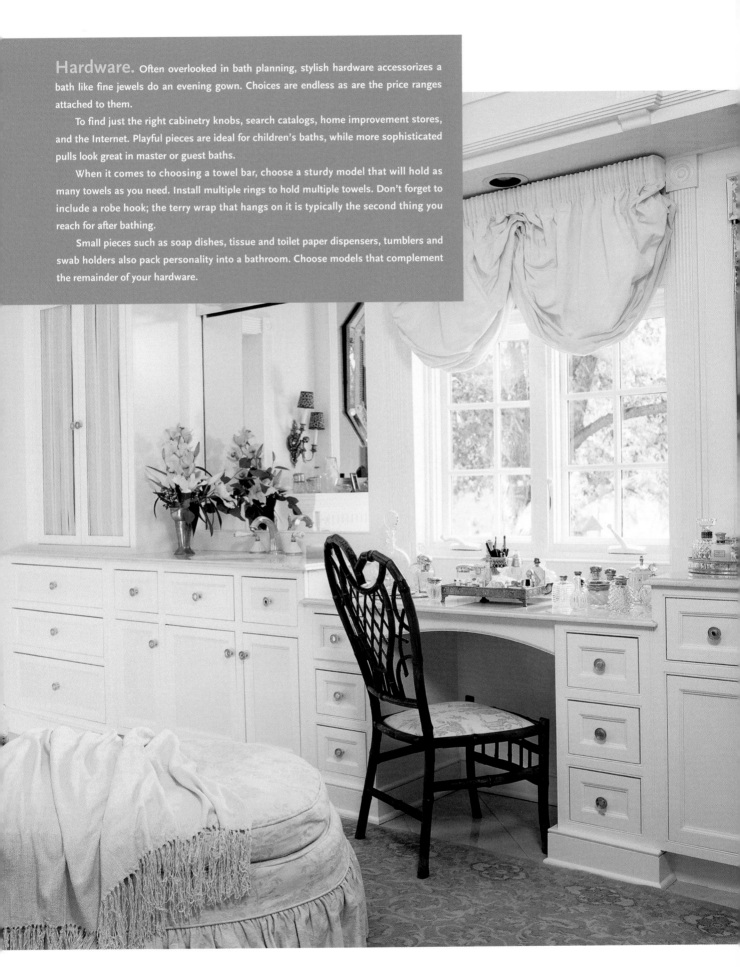

Hardware. Often overlooked in bath planning, stylish hardware accessorizes a bath like fine jewels do an evening gown. Choices are endless as are the price ranges attached to them.

To find just the right cabinetry knobs, search catalogs, home improvement stores, and the Internet. Playful pieces are ideal for children's baths, while more sophisticated pulls look great in master or guest baths.

When it comes to choosing a towel bar, choose a sturdy model that will hold as many towels as you need. Install multiple rings to hold multiple towels. Don't forget to include a robe hook; the terry wrap that hangs on it is typically the second thing you reach for after bathing.

Small pieces such as soap dishes, tissue and toilet paper dispensers, tumblers and swab holders also pack personality into a bathroom. Choose models that complement the remainder of your hardware.

furnishings and accessories

FREESTANDING FURNITURE

If you love the look of fine furniture and like the idea of converting a bedroom dresser into a vanity base, consider converting a sideboard or dining hutch into a vanity. The antique Dutch klapbuffet, *opposite*, now serves as a vanity. In the same bathroom, a mahogany bookcase serves as display and storage space. When you grow tired of a freestanding furniture piece, there's no need to redo the entire bathroom; you can swap the individual piece for something new.

Unite distinctly different vanities by visually connecting them with matching or complementary faucets and sinks. Likewise, mount similar mirrors and sconces above each vanity. Don't be afraid to vary vanity heights to fit the individual needs of each user; 36-inch-high vanities are more comfortable for people over 5 feet 8 inches tall, while 30-inch-high vanities are more comfortable for people of smaller stature.

Fit vanities on opposite or perpendicular walls to help solve traffic-flow problems that can occur when two people must share the space at the same time.

A WELL-FURNISHED BATH

With an upholstered chair, side table, and a few thoughtfully selected accessories, you can turn up the comfort level in your bath. Carve out a small sitting area in a corner of the room. Think of the tub as a sofa and position the other furnishings accordingly. If you enjoy a cup of tea and the morning paper each day, for example, plan for task lighting in the sitting area. Tuck in a multi-shelved table with space for reading materials, cup and saucer, and whatever else you need for comfort.

If a sitting area for reading isn't your idea of a soothing retreat, consider

ABOVE: **Create a signature piece in your bath by converting a piece of furniture into a vanity. Here a Dutch antique klapbuffet hosts a stainless-steel vessel sink.**

OPPOSITE: **Create display space in your bath for favorite objects and bath oils, salts, and scrubs.**

Designer Tip

Glass-front doors transform standard storage into display space, but the glass also put limits on what can be stored there. Rolled towels, fancy soaps, and perfume bottles look great, but it is not practical to fill every wall cabinet with them.

To create the look of a glass-front door without the necessity of neatness, use mirrored or frosted glass instead of clear-glass panels. The look is equally appealing and your storage options are not compromised.

including a television to catch up on the day's news. Create a recessed niche to house the set where it's visible from the tub but out of the way; or mount it in a corner near the ceiling where it can be viewed from several areas in the room.

Decorate the room. Though you want to be conscientious of the potential humidity levels in a bathroom, the space shouldn't be devoid of art and accessories. Hang framed prints, shelves, and small cabinets above toilets, between windows, over doors, and in open wall expanses. Create an overall design scheme for a unified look.

Use cut flowers or houseplants for a fresh look. Many potted plants will thrive in the bathroom, depending on the light conditions.

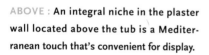

ABOVE : An integral niche in the plaster wall located above the tub is a Mediterranean touch that's convenient for display.

ABOVE RIGHT: Hooks offer a stylish and less space-consuming alternative to towel bars.

RIGHT: This bath "parlor" integrates living-room style furnishings such as rugs, lamps, and an antique settee with more traditional bath fixtures.

OPPOSITE: This shapely chair—slipcovered in bath towels—provides kick-back comfort in the corner of a master suite overlooking a garden.

Designer Tip

Carve out a spot for a coffee service in the bathroom. You'll relish the comfort of starting or ending the day in the solitude of your own space. For true luxury, include refrigerated drawers, espresso maker, sink, and storage for cups and saucers.

everything in its place

Once you've selected materials, position fixtures comfortably and provide for lighting, ventilation, and organizational systems in your new bath. »

>> Remodeling success is measured in terms of comfort, function, and personal style. Ergonomics plays a significant role in bath design. So do plumbing layouts and safety. Design and building professionals can assist in making your dreams become a successful reality. Here, you'll also find ways to stylishly organize and store everything in your bath, all while ensuring your bath is as easy on the eyes as it is on the body.

space guidelines

Based on average human measurements and needs, professional designers have developed recommendations for minimum clearance around doors, fixtures, cabinets, and other common bathroom elements. The following guidelines outlined by the National Kitchen and Bath Association (NKBA) should work well for anyone at any stage of life, although some of these dimensions will need to be larger for a completely barrier-free bath, as described on pages 130–133. Keep in mind that these are the recommended minimums, not hard and fast rules; allow more space if the fit seems tight for any of the bathroom's intended users.

FLOOR SPACE GUIDELINES

Universal design standards recommend leaving at least 30×48 inches of clear floor space in front of each fixture. Clear floor spaces suggested at each fixture may overlap. That is, you can add the clear space between a toilet and a tub together, just make sure that the amount of space between the two meets the minimum guidelines for both.

Door openings. Doorways should be at least 32 inches wide. Allow clear floor space at least the width of the door on the push side and a larger clear floor space on the pull side to allow room for bath users to comfortably open, close, and pass through the doorway.

Walkways. Make passages between the bathroom walls and fixtures at least 36 inches wide.

LEFT: Make sure to leave enough clearance between dual sinks so that two people can comfortably use the sinks at the same time. In addition to having more than the minimum recommended eight inches of counter space between sinks, this vanity features a middle set of drawers between the sinks to define the grooming areas and provide additional storage.

OPPOSITE: With an adjacent tub and shower, leave plenty of room to enter both fixtures. Notice that even with the shower door open there is plenty of clearance to enter the tub and exit the shower.

Sink Fronts. Leave a minimum of 30 inches of clear floor space in front of each sink. To meet universal design standards of 30×48 inches, if there is open knee space under the sink, up to 12 of the 48 inches can extend beneath the sink.

Toilet allowance. Leave a clear floor space of 30 inches in front of the toilet. Leave at least 16 inches of space from the centerline of the fixture to the closest fixture or sidewall. If you plan to install a toilet in its own separate compartment, make the compartment at least 36 inches wide and 66 inches long. Install a swing-out door or a pocket door on the opening to the compartment. The doorway should be at least 32 inches wide.

Bidet allowance. Leave a clear floor space of 30 inches in front of the bidet. Leave at least 18 inches of space from the centerline of the fixture to the closest fixture or sidewall. When the toilet and bidet are adjacent, maintain the 18 inches of minimum clearance to all obstructions. Follow toilet allowance guidelines for a combination bidet/toilet unit.

Bathtub entrance. Plan a 30-inch section of clear space adjacent to the length of the tub if you'll approach the fixture from the side.

Shower entrance. For showers less than 60 inches wide, plan a clear floor space that is 36 inches deep and 12 inches wider than the shower. For wider showers, plan for a clear floor space that is 36 inches deep and as wide as the shower.

Shower interior. The minimum usable interior dimensions, measured from wall to wall, are 36×36 inches, but some people prefer more room. If there simply isn't enough space, you can reduce this to 32×32 inches, but it may make the shower uncomfortable for many users. Design the shower doors so

that they open into the bathroom—not into the stall—to avoid crowding the space in the shower.

Shower and tub controls. Position controls so that you can reach them from inside as well as outside of the shower and tub.

GROOMING SPACE GUIDELINES

These NKBA guidelines ensure that everyone in the bath has adequate grooming space and elbowroom near the sink, vanities, and countertops.

Sink space. Leave at least 15 inches of clearance from the centerline of a sink to the closest sidewall. If you are including two sinks in a vanity, leave at least 30 inches of clearance between the centerlines of each. If the sinks are wider than 30 inches, increase the distance by several inches to provide a minimum of 8 inches of open counter space between the sinks to allow adequate elbowroom when both sinks are in use.

Vanity height. If you are including two vanities, consider positioning them at different heights—between 32 and 43 inches high—to match the comfort level of the people who use them. Vanity cabinets are typically 30 to 32 inches high, while kitchen base cabinets are typically 36 inches high. Many people find the 36-

inch height more comfortable for standing. If space allows, add a 30-inch-high section with knee space below for sitting.

Mirror height. Locate a mirror above a vanity so that it is at approximate eye level for the primary users. If the top of the mirror is tilted away from the wall, the mirror can be positioned higher above the floor.

Door and drawer widths. When designing a vanity cabinet, split doors in cabinets that are 24 inches or wider. Large single doors can be awkward to open, especially in a narrow bathroom. Avoid narrow doors and drawers. Nine-inch widths generally are too narrow to be extremely useful.

Corner comfort. To eliminate sharp corners, use countertops with rounded corners and eased edges.

OPPOSITE: **The space between the vanity and tub serves as a walkway to the sitting area and toilet compartment in this bath. Allowing plenty of room for foot traffic through the bath as well as space in front of the vanity and tub ensures comfortable morning routines.**

ABOVE: **For maximum comfort, allow ample space between a toilet and the fixtures on either side.**

barrier-free design

The goal of a barrier-free bath is to make all users as independent and as comfortable as possible. Even if no one in your home has special needs now, planning a bath that can accommodate wheelchairs and walkers can make guests—or even a kid with a cast—feel more welcome and more comfortable.

Location, location, location. Creating a barrier-free bath starts first with the room's location. It should be situated on the home's ground floor so that there are no stairs to climb up or down.

Door size. Plan for a clear door opening of 34 inches; larger openings are difficult to open and close from a seated position and narrower openings make it difficult, if not impossible, for a wheelchair to make it through.

Handle selection. Equip entrance doors, drawers, and faucets with lever or D-shape handles. They are easier to operate than knobs, especially for young children and people with arthritis or limited mobility.

Floor space. For a typical-size wheelchair to make a complete turnaround, you'll need to leave a circular area of clear floor space measuring 5 feet in diameter. Leave an area in front of the sink that measures at least 30x48 inches (although the clear floor space can overlap with other fixtures). Toilets need a clear floor space that is 48 inches square. Bathtubs need a clear floor space of 60x60 inches in front of the tub.

Shower stalls. Shower stalls are easier to get into and out of than bathtubs. Choose a stall with no curb or a very short one. Slope the floor toward the drain to ensure that the water stays within the enclosures. Shower stalls need to measure at least 4 feet square with an opening that is at least 36 inches wide. Include a built-in bench or seat

that is 17 to 19 inches above the floor, grab bars, a single-handle lever control, and a handheld shower spray.

Bathtubs. If a tub is a necessity, install grab bars in the tub along the sidewall and the two end walls. Install the bars 33 to 36 inches above the tub bottom and another set 9 inches above

the tub rim. All bars should be at least 24 inches long.

Knee space. The knee space under a sink should be about 27 inches high and 30 inches wide. In addition, hot water pipes should be insulated or concealed to protect users from scalding.

OPPOSITE: With no door or threshold, the shower allows a wheelchair user to roll in and transfer to a bench for showering. The bench is designed for stability.

ABOVE: A shallow vitreous-china sink is designed to provide extra knee space below for easy wheelchair access. The large faucet handles at the vanity sink and in the shower allow for easy grasping. Bars flanking the toilet can be turned to hang flat against the wall when not in use. The cabinet provides handy storage, and its drawers roll open easily.

LEFT: The sink drain is at the back corner of the sink, allowing the pipes below to be installed out of the way of someone in a wheelchair.

Barrier-Free Information:
- Center for Universal Design, North Carolina State University; 50 Pullen Road, Brooks Hall, Room 104, Campus Box 8613, Raleigh, NC 27695-8613; 800/647-6777; www.design.ncsu.edu/cud
- Abledata; 8630 Fenton Street, Suite 930, Silver Spring, MD 20910; 800/227-0216; www.abledata.com

LEFT: This freestanding shower bench offers more flexibility than a built-in version. It's designed not to tip over. Reinforcements in the walls enable the grab bars to bear significant weight. Large faucet handles simplify grasping. Two showerheads allow water to spray at practically any height.

Toilet talk. The ideal placement for a toilet is in a corner of the bath so that you can install grab bars both behind the toilet and next to it. Leave at least 48 inches of clear floor space to either one side or in front of the toilet. A toilet 3 inches higher than a conventional model makes it easier to transfer to or from a wheelchair. As a general rule, grab bars should be 33 to 36 inches above the floor. They should be 42 inches long on a sidewall and not more than 12 inches from the back wall. The bar on the back wall should be at least 24 inches long and extend at least 12 inches from each side of the center of the toilet.

Grab bars. Rated to withstand up to 300 pounds of pressure, grab bars are efficient only if they are attached securely. Secure grab bars to wall studs, or if possible, before putting up drywall, install ¾-inch plywood sheathing over the studs from floor to ceiling. You can then install bars anywhere on the walls

For Safety's Sake. **Grab bars.** Reinforce walls for grab bars at the time of construction. Install grab bars in the tub, shower, and toilet areas. **GFCI outlets.** Protect all receptacles, lights, and switches in the room with ground fault circuit interrupters (GFCIs) to reduce the risk of electrical shocks. Install only moistureproof light fixtures above the tub and shower areas. **Flooring grip.** Install only slip-resistant flooring throughout the entire bath area. Choose rugs with nonskid backing, and install rubber foot pads on all step stools and vanity chairs to prevent them from slipping when in use. **Shower and tub surround safety.** Include a bench or a seat that is 17 to 19 inches above the floor and at least 15 inches deep. It can be a hanging or folding seat; to support the seat, you will need to reinforce the wall when you install the surround. To reduce the risk of falls, avoid installing steps for climbing into the shower or tub. Design the surround so that you can reach the controls from inside and outside the stall. Put the controls 38 to 48 inches above the floor and above the grab bar if there is one. Locate the controls between the showerhead and the stall door. For a handheld showerhead model, locate the head no higher than 48 inches above the floor when in its lowest position. To help prevent cuts and bruises, add a cushion to the tub spout. (Waterproof cushions in various shapes are readily available at many bath and hardware centers.) Install only laminated safety glass with a plastic inner layer, tempered glass, or approved plastic for any clear face of a shower or tub enclosure or partition that reaches to within 18 inches of the floor. **Water safety.** Turn your hot water heater down to 120 degrees. Or install a pressure-balancing/temperature regulator or a temperature-limiting device for all faucet heads, particularly showerheads, to prevent scalding. To prevent drowning, never leave a small child unattended in the bathtub. Keep washcloths and toys at tubside, so you won't be tempted to walk away for any reason. Install a childproof latch on the toilet lid. Round all countertop and cabinetry corners. **Safety latches.** Finally, if you EVER have young children in your house, install childproof locks on all cabinets.

as needed. Buy bars with a nonslip texture. They come in a variety of colors and styles to blend with most any bath decor.

Windows. Casement windows are the easiest to operate from a wheelchair. Install windows 24 to 30 inches above the floor so that wheelchair users can open, close, and easily see out of them.

LEFT: A pulley system and crank allow the mirror to hang flat against the wall or to be tilted downward to accommodate someone who is seated.

BELOW: These support bars offer upper and lower handles. A child who uses a wheelchair can use the lower handle for support when transferring. As the child grows, the upper support will be the correct height, so the bars never need to be adjusted. The supports can be folded flat against the wall when not in use. In this bathroom, extra structural supports were installed in the ceiling above the tub so as the child grows and gets heavier, a lift can be installed to assist in transferring him or her in and out of the tub.

lighting

Proper bath lighting provides shadowless, glare-free illumination throughout the room. Plan for a blend of at least two different illumination strategies: ambient and task lighting. Consider including a third type of illumination: accent lighting. Provide separate controls for each type of lighting.

Ambient or general lighting creates a uniform, overall glow in the entire bath space and comes from one or more, usually overhead, sources. (If your bath is larger than 35 square feet, one overhead fixture will not be enough.) Backing up this general lighting plan is task lighting. These fixtures are positioned to eliminate shadows in the areas where you perform specific tasks, such as applying makeup, shaving, or taking a bath. Accent lighting occurs when you aim light on an object or surface simply to show it off. For this job, you'll need a lightbulb—or lamp—with a beam that is three to five times brighter than the general lighting lamps. To learn what types of lighting are inherently brighter, research what's available in incandescent, fluorescent, or halogen bulbs, how the lights can be installed, and then pair them with an almost endless variety of fixture styles.

FIXTURE STYLES

There are many fixture choices. You will likely need a combination of styles to fully light your bath.

Recessed downlights. Also called can lights, these lights are very popular and the least-obtrusive fixture for general or task lighting. For best ambient lighting, position these lights close enough together so that their light patterns overlap.

Pendant lights. Lights that hang from a wire, rod, or chain can work well in the bathroom, either as overall ambient light or placed over the vanity for task lighting. If you have a large traditional-style bath, a small chandelier also can give the bath the look and feel of living space as opposed to a utility room.

Surface-mount fixtures. These fixtures work well in bathrooms that cannot accommodate recessed fixtures, a common problem in bath remodelings. Available in many styles and sizes, there are surface-mount fixtures for either incandescent or fluorescent bulbs.

Wall sconces. To create ambient lighting, use wall sconces throughout the bath. Wall sconces placed on both sides of a mirror offer shadow-free task light for applying makeup and shaving.

Shower fixtures. For safety purposes, shower fixtures should always be waterproof and steamproof; most building codes require this.

Rheostats. Also called dimmers, these light-regulating knobs, switches, or levers enable you to set the fixture at any level of light from a soft glow that backs up a candlelit bath to radiant brightness for cleaning the tub afterward. Dimmers are also energy savers as they enable you to use only the amount of light you need and not more.

LIGHTING THE MIRROR

Because your bathroom mirror serves as the primary grooming center in the house, make sure it is evenly illuminated and free of shadows. To do this, light sources need to be placed so that the light is evenly distributed from above, below, and both sides. This cross-lighting prevents shadows—which make applying makeup evenly difficult.

Bulb Basics. Incandescent. Introduced by Thomas Edison back in 1879, incandescent bulbs are still widely used and appreciated for the white light they offer, and because more energy-efficient, longer lasting incandescents are available today. Low-voltage incandescent fixtures make good accent lighting. Operating on 12 or 24 volts, these lights require transformers, which are sometimes built into the fixture to step down the voltage from standard 120-volt household circuits. **Fluorescent.** Fluorescent tubes are energy efficient and last far longer than incandescent bulbs. Today's tubes reduce noise and flicker and come in a wide spectrum of colors. New subcompact tubes can be used in fixtures that usually require incandescent bulbs. **Halogen.** Quartz halogen lights offer bright, white light good for task or accent lighting. Usually low-voltage, these bulbs do put off a large amount of heat. Choose a fixture specifically designed for halogen bulbs.

RIGHT: **Include a variety of light sources for a well-lit bath. Recessed halogens above the sink and on both sides of the vanity provide task lighting. Accent lights at each side of the mirror eliminate harsh shadows. An overhead fixture provides ambient light.**

that they fully light the tub or shower but don't shine directly in your eyes when you're relaxing in the tub. All light switches should be located at least 6 feet from a tub or shower.

STALL LIGHTING

One centrally located fixture, installed in the ceiling or high on the wall, should be enough to adequately light a shower stall.

NIGHT-LIGHTS

Night-lights make those late-night or early-morning trips to the bathroom more comfortable for people of all ages. For an easy, affordable solution, plug in an automatic night-light that senses the amount of light coming into the room. Or install a low-voltage system below the vanity toe-kick or around some shelving to provide soft nighttime illumination.

OPPOSITE: **Incandescent tubes of lighting provide flattering sidelight at these vanities and avoid shadows that overhead lights would create.**

ABOVE: **The shape of the fixture in the shower stall is similar to the surface-mount fixtures above the twin basins. These fixtures are mounted close to the mirror to highlight the face of a person standing in front of the counter. Centering the fixtures above the sinks gives even lighting from both sides.**

Plan to install one or two fixtures above the mirror that cast light just over the front edge of the sink and the countertop. Add two additional lights centered on each side of the mirror at eye level. If there is not enough space at the sides of the mirror for fixtures, you can create cross-lighting by making the light above the mirror longer than the width of the mirror itself. Choose a light color countertop (preferably white) so that m ore light reflects on your face.

Although the trend to design soothing spalike retreats makes them less common, "movie star" lights—the kind you see in the dressing rooms of actors—

that surround the entire mirror with bulbs are an ideal lighting solution for perfect makeup application.

No matter your approach to mirror lighting, always select bulbs designed for vanity illumination: These bulbs create light in the daylight spectrum range. Avoid choosing bulbs that are too white or too yellow in color as the mirror won't reflect a true picture of how you look outside the bathroom.

LIGHTING THE SHOWER AND TUB

In an enclosed shower or tub area, most building codes require enclosed, vapor-proof downlights. Place the fixtures so

windows

Proper lighting goes beyond choosing the right fixtures; it also includes bringing in as much natural light as possible with windows, skylights, glass doors, wall cutouts, and glass block. Mirrors also reflect and increase the amount of natural light that enters your bath.

Window selection and placement, in particular, are key to creating a visually pleasing bath with adequate ventilation. Think beyond the outdated notion of using a single double-hung window. Look for places to install additional windows where they will shed more light in the vanity area without looking out of

place in your home's exterior. Consider installing a frosted-glass door or an open cutout between the master bath and bedroom to let light filter from one room into the other.

Let your room's proportions and features dictate window size. Windows intended to accent a tub, for example, look best when they are large enough to line up with architectural features—such as matching windows to a tub's width—and each other.

Window placement impacts privacy and the flow of natural light. To maximize airflow, place two or more operable

windows on opposite or adjacent walls. Placing windows high on a wall is a useful technique when you want to introduce light to an area without compromising privacy. If views are prime and your home secluded, surround a soaking tub bay with windows so you can enjoy the surroundings while you indulge in a soothing bath.

If wall space is limited, or views are less than appealing, try a skylight. Operable models offer ventilation as well as natural light. Sky windows have frames that match wall windows. Skylights offer an ideal way to bring daylight into a bath, providing your bath's location allows for it. To prevent moisture and condensation problems, choose a high-quality model and install it according to the manufacturer's specifications.

OPPOSITE: **A dramatic three-pane skylight floods this bath with light. Operable skylights are another option that provide both sunlight and ventilation without sacrificing privacy.**

LEFT: **Operable lower windows combine with a decorative arched upper window to open up this bath to natural light and ventilation. Shutters on the lower windows provide privacy.**

Designer Tip

If you're remodeling your existing bath, try to stick with the predominate window type used in the rest of the house. Swapping window types or styles creates a patchwork look on your home's exterior.

ventilation

Without proper ventilation, the ceiling may mildew, the wallpaper may curl, the paint may peel, and the mirror may even begin to deteriorate. Open windows when you can and supplement them with a high-quality fan.

To determine the size of venting fan you need, measure your bath's cubic feet (width times length times ceiling height) and multiply the result by 8, then divide by 60. The result is the minimum cubic feet per minute (cfm) rating you'll need in a venting fan. The noise from a fan will resonate on the hard surfaces of a bathroom, so choose a quiet fan that vents to the outside with a noise level not exceeding 3 sones; less than 2 sones is highly recommended.

BELOW: **Install operable windows—such as these casement windows—to add ventilation throughout the bath.**

water systems

WATER CONSERVATION

Clean, fresh water is a renewable resource, but we must use it wisely to keep supply and demand in equilibrium. All states now require that newly installed toilets be low-flow fixtures. (See pages 114–115 for more information on low-flow toilets.)

Showers are another heavy water user. Low-flow showerheads restrict water output to 2.5 gallons of water per minute. That's 30 to 60 percent less than an average showerhead output. The technology of water-saving showerheads has improved to the point where many of today's low-cost models seem just as generous with water as their older higher-consuming counterparts, so you won't feel as if you're making a sacrifice when you're in the shower. Flow-restricting aerators on sink faucets aid conservation still further. All these low-flow fixtures are available in hardware stores, home centers, and bath fixture shops.

FILTRATION SYSTEMS

Water that contains a significant amount of iron, sulfur, lime, and other mineral impurities is commonly referred to as hard water. Hard water can irritate the skin, causing itching and dryness, particularly in the winter months when the air is drier. Hard water also causes unsightly deposits on your fixtures and can affect how well your shampoos and soaps lather.

Bacteria, nitrates, lead, and other contaminants can make your water unsafe for drinking. Do-it-yourself water-testing kits that cost about $20 (available at home centers and via the Internet) can check for both hardness and contamination. If your water test shows problems other than hardness,

contact your local water municipality immediately to determine what steps you need to take. A water purification system may be necessary. If your water is determined to be hard, you might want to invest in a water softener. Softened water requires less soap for bathing and your plumbing system will work more smoothly because your water heater, pipes, showerheads, and faucets won't collect the corrosive scale that hard water causes.

ABOVE: **Showers and toilets are potential heavy water users. New showerheads offer luxurious bathing options and conserve water. New low-flow toilets contain efficient operating mechanisms.**

organization strategies

The key to keeping a bath neat and tidy is to make putting something away as easy as leaving it out on the counter. Being organized saves you time, space, and money while adding simplicity to your life.

Take inventory. To have enough room for everything you need, you need to get rid of what you never use. Sort through those bottles at the back of the cabinet and throw out what you never use or don't like. Some products, such as suntan lotions and face creams, have expiration dates. Throw out items that have expired and start out fresh.

Designate a specific place for each and every thing. You'll be more likely to put things back where they belong

LEFT AND BELOW: **Take cues from the kitchen to boost your bath's storage potential. Here a pair of 4-inch-wide pullout units store bath essentials while a large, binlike drawer with air holes collects dirty laundry.**

Easy-clean sinks. When selecting a sink for your bath, consider how much use the room will get and who will use it. If it will be the main bath for several active children, an easy-to-clean sink is more critical than if you're remodeling a showy powder room that receives only occasional use.

How your sink is attached to the countertop affects ease of cleaning. Integral sinks have no seams. Undermount sinks are attached to the underside of a countertop. Both integral and undermount types make it easy to wipe messes from the counter right into the sink. Self-rimming sinks, on the other hand, have a perimeter lip that's sealed with a bead of caulk that can be a dirt collector.

and less likely to unknowingly duplicate items if you know exactly where each item belongs.

Store it where you use it. Whenever possible, you should store items right where they are used. For example, store your hair dryer in an appliance garage where you can keep it plugged in and ready to use. Store your toothbrush, toothpaste, and mouthwash close enough to the sink so that you can grab them without even looking or taking a step away from the sink.

Assign everything else a space based on frequency of use. Store items

used for special occasions at the back of the cabinet or in a pantry cabinet down the hall. Store your cleaning supplies below the sink.

OPPOSITE: **This custom vanity features a towel bar convenient to the sink and a shelf beneath for folded towels. A nearby niche with shelves keeps toiletries tidy.**

ABOVE LEFT: **This bath offers three ideas for displaying and storing towels beyond the typical towel bar. Add door hooks to the back of the bathroom door for towels and robes. For display, place rolled towels in a**

wire or wicker wall basket. A ladder featuring chipped paint, fit for a cottage look, offers drying space for multiple towels.

TOP RIGHT: **Claim shallow or narrow spaces. This slim closet between a door and a vanity creates the perfect storage tower for bath essentials. When its door is closed, a full-length mirror provides a reflection and the illusion of more space.**

BOTTOM RIGHT: **A cabinet door reveals a slide-out hamper. Look for built-in hamper designs that allow you to easily remove the hamper for toting to the washer and dryer.**

Keep it simple. When you have to open a door, stoop down, and reach to the back of a base cabinet to get to something you use every day, chances are you won't take the time to put it away when you're finished using it. Store the items you use frequently in the most convenient locations so that you will be more inclined to put them away.

Make it comfortable. It is easier on your back to reach into a drawer and

grab a towel than it is to bend down and pull one out of a cabinet. Small vanity drawers, however, may only be big enough to hold one spare towel. Consider installing pullouts for towel storage. For safety purposes, in freestanding vanities store heavier items in the lower spots, and lighter items in the high ones.

Put wasted space to work. Equip false sink fronts with pull-down baskets to hold toothpastes, razors, and other

ABOVE: **A chrome rack with a shelf centralizes towel storage just above the tub for convenience.**

OPPOSITE: **You don't have to sacrifice storage in a small bathroom. This custom-built cabinet was placed on an angle to avoid making the entry to the bath feel cramped. The cabinet, with glass doors, a drawer, and a pullout hamper, packs plenty of storage in a small amount of space.**

Easy Cleaning. Part of maintaining a well-organized bath is preventing your dream bath from becoming a cleaning nightmare. Including these features will help.

Cut down on wiping up. Consider fog-free mirrors and automatic or lever-handle faucets. Choose nonporous stone, laminate, or solid-surface walls, floors, and countertops. The fewer the seams, nooks, or crannies, the better. Curving your countertop up the wall creates a seamless backsplash that eliminates the dirt-catching right-angle joint where the counter meets the wall. In front, make sure the countertop edge overhangs the cabinet doors or drawers somewhat; otherwise spills may get into the cabinets or seep into drawers. Likewise, the fewer the seams or gaps in your floor, the fewer the places for dirt and hair to collect. Eliminate the seam between the base cabinet and the vertical surface of the toe-kick by "rolling" the edge of the floor up to the top of the toe-kick, replacing the right angle joint with a smooth curve. The technique is easiest with vinyl, linoleum, or tile, but it is also possible with wood if you have the edge pieces custom milled.

Reduce mildew. To keep germs and mildew at bay, look for the following products: moisture-resistant tile underlayment, mildew-resistant tile grout, mildew-resistant wall paint, and antibacterial or bacteria-inhibiting features (some manufacturers of shower stalls and tub surrounds, for example, incorporate microban protection into their gel-coated interiors).

small items. Cut a niche between wall studs to hold perfume bottles, lotions, and powders. Add narrow shelves to the backside of base cabinet doors to hold additional lightweight toiletry items.

Add a parking place. Add a built-in bench where you can sit to pull on socks and shoes. Install drawers below the bench to hold socks and undergarments so you can quickly dress after a bath or shower.

Create a spot for dirty clothes. Is your bath situated next to the laundry

room? If so, install a small top-swing door between the two rooms so you can toss clothes directly into a hamper stored on the laundry room side. If the laundry is below the bath, add a clothes chute so you don't have to tote dirty laundry down the stairs. If neither of these is an option, add a built-in hamper that is large enough to store the amount of dirty clothes that usually gather before you wash a load.

Commit to a clutter-free bath. Once you have your belongings in your cabinets, you'll have to work to keep the new system in place. Don't fill every single spot; keep a few drawers open for new items. If storage space is limited, follow this rule: one new thing in, one old thing out.

ALL PHOTOS: **If you have the wall space, don't limit storage to a conventional vanity with only a few shelves and drawers. Floor-to-ceiling cabinets offer storage at many levels. Drawers above the countertop organize small essentials for at-a-glance ease. Shelves placed between head and waist level are especially convenient if you groom while standing. To decoratively camouflage grooming supplies, consider glass doors with fabric panels such as these. Small rods on the inside of the doors hold the sheers in place at the top and the bottom. Cabinets near the ceiling and below counter level are ideal for lesser-used items, such as extra makeup bags.**

LEFT: Use storage accessories that complement the style of your bath. Here a three-tier bamboo shelf contains necessities.

RIGHT TOP AND BOTTOM: Instead of a conventional medicine cabinet above, narrow storage units flank the sink. Open cubbyholes keep towels close at hand.

BELOW: Take advantage of the space between studs to create recessed shelves for much-needed storage space in small bathrooms.

working
with professionals

Once you have carefully thought through your bath plans, you're heading into the homestretch. Before you begin the construction work, here are details you'll need to know about the process.

Hiring a skilled, dependable contractor is the most important step toward carrying out your remodeling plan in a timely, gratifying, and cost-effective manner. There are several kinds of contractors, so you'll want to match your remodeling needs with the capabilities of the people you hire to handle the project. Remodeling workers fall into six general categories:

Repair workers. These are the jacks-of-all-trades who do a little bit of everything from carpentry to minor plumbing and painting. These workers can be just right for small jobs, such as replacing a door or adding a window. They charge less per hour than specialized tradespeople.

Tradespeople. When you have a larger remodeling project, but one that involves only a single trade, such as plumbing, electrical work, or carpentry, you can save money by hiring these tradespeople yourself. If you are interested in just a new sink, for example,

hire a reputable plumber. Most skilled tradespeople can handle the entire job themselves even if there's a little carpentry involved. If they don't have the tools to do the entire job, most can let you know who else you need to contact.

General contractors. For projects that require several specialized tradespeople, you may want to hire a general remodeling contractor. This person or company will manage the entire project from start to finish. You'll get a single bid, and you won't have to hire or schedule all the required subcontractors. Your overall costs will be somewhat higher

OPPOSITE: During the planning stage of this luxurious bath, the homeowners could not figure out how to add a sizeable master bath. An architect and a residential designer provided the solution of adding on over the sunroom. Reinforcement was added to support the weighty fixtures.

ABOVE: To add modern conveniences while remaining respectful of the original 1950s styling, one of the original architects of the house and an interior designer and architectural historian updated this bath as part of a whole-house makeover.

Permits. Don't forget to contact your local municipality and county building departments to see what permits are required for your project. If your plans are limited to changing surface materials, you probably won't need a permit. If you'll be making changes to your home's plumbing or electrical systems, you'll probably need one.

because you will pay something for the contractor's labor, but if the contractor is a good one, you'll save yourself time, headaches, and the glitches that could arise from coordinating product delivery and tradespeople.

Architects. These professionals are experienced at drawing up plans to determine how best to use the space you have. You can also hire an architect by the hour to look over the plans you have, or you can pay one to draw up your plan from scratch.

Interior designers. These professionals also draw up plans and offer ideas on how best to use your space. You also can hire a designer to look over existing plans to have them make recommendations for improved use of space or smarter selections.

NKBA-certified designers. Professionals with this certification have passed courses from the trade organizations; it's another level of assurance when you're hiring help.

HIRING A CONTRACTOR

Finding a good contractor and establishing an effective working relationship are key to a successful remodeling project. Use the following tips to choose professionals wisely:

Get the names of several contractors. In addition to asking for recommendations from your friends, solicit recommendations from your architect or designer, colleagues at work, a home-improvement loan officer at a local bank, or even a trusted employee of a hardware store or a home-improvement center.

Get rough estimates from any and all contractors who interest you. A rough estimate isn't a precise bid, but getting several general estimates at this stage will give you some idea of how straightforward those contractors are when the subject turns to money.

Before calling any contractor back to ask for a final bid, obtain additional references and check them all. Check with your local Better Business Bureau (BBB) to see if complaints are outstanding against any finalists. Also see if she or he is a member of the BBB. If so and there are problems, you can use the BBB's alternative dispute resolution services.

Narrow your list of candidates to no more than five and no fewer than three contractors.

Get at least three bids. Ask to have the bids by a certain date, allowing contractors about three weeks. Receiving the bid in time will give you an indication of the contractor's time-management skills.

Review all the bids carefully. Some may be more inclusive than others, so make sure you are comparing like bids. Quality contractors use top-grade materials and hire skilled tradespeople; this is reflected in their bids. Regard a bid that comes in much lower than the others with healthy skepticism.

Don't base your decision on the bid alone. In the long run, a good working relationship with a contractor and satisfaction with his or her work is worth a few extra dollars.

Do not make the last payment to a contractor until you're satisfied that all subcontractors and suppliers have been paid—ask to see written proof. Have the job checked by a local municipality to make sure it passes building inspection.

Finally, walk through the completed project with your contractor and agree that the job is complete.

BELOW: **One goal in this remodel was increased ceiling height but code restrictions prohibited a higher roof. An architect used scissored trusses to achieve the goal.**

bath planning kit

To transform your bath dreams into reality, consider all the details. Sketch out some ideas of your own, even if you will work with a bath designer. Doing so is recommended because your drawings provide insight into what you're after. Use the bath planning kit on the following pages to work through the process.

To help you consider how you'll use your new bath, visualize how the room's various zones—washing, bathing, toilet, storage, and perhaps sitting, exercising, or even snacking—relate to one another. Figure out where you'd like these various zones to go and how the bath relates to the surrounding rooms such as bedrooms, walk-in closets, dressing rooms, halls, or sitting rooms. Finally, consider which architectural features you'd like to add or highlight and what types, sizes, and styles of fixtures, cabinetry, shelving, and furniture you want to include.

Plot the space using the grids on page 158. One square equals 1 square foot of floor space. Plot your bath, including any adjacent closet, dressing room, hall, bedroom, sitting, snacking areas, or bump-outs you'd like to add or remodel at the same time. One of the keys to making your bath both functional and beautiful is good placement of doors, windows, fixtures, cabinetry, and built-in features such as shelving or towel warmers.

Use the architectural symbols to mark the position of existing architectural features. Use a different color to indicate added features such as the placement of built-ins and new fixtures. Use dotted lines to mark obstructions, including prominent light fixtures and angled ceilings. If you're building a new addition, mark the existing structure in one color and use a different one to mark the addition.

Use the templates to experiment with different placements for fixtures, cabinetry, and built-in features. Trace or photocopy the appropriate items from the templates on the following pages and cut them out with a crafts knife or scissors. If you have furniture or special features such as a reading chair or exercise equipment that you'd like to include in your new bath, measure and draw them to the same scale on the grid paper.

TEMPLATE TIME

Use these templates to mark the placement of common bathroom components. The templates include a plan-view (top-down) perspective, allowing you to create floor plans. Most bath components are represented here, including various types and sizes of sinks, cabinets, showers, toilets, bidets, tubs, and more. Pay attention to details such as door swings and drawer extensions as you consider the placment of these items in the room. If you don't see a template for something you'd like to include, draw your own.

PLANNING GRID

Use a photocopier to reproduce the grid at its original size, then cut out the templates on pages 156–157 to design your bathroom. Grid scale: 1 square equals 1 square foot.

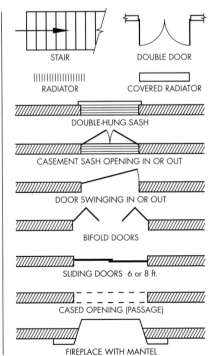

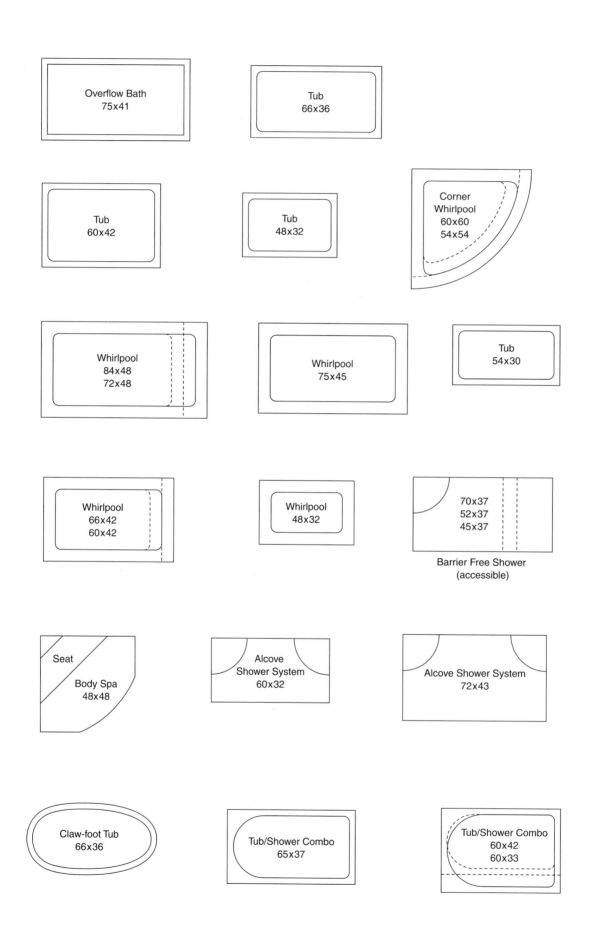

Overflow Bath
75x41

Tub
66x36

Tub
60x42

Tub
48x32

Corner
Whirlpool
60x60
54x54

Whirlpool
84x48
72x48

Whirlpool
75x45

Tub
54x30

Whirlpool
66x42
60x42

Whirlpool
48x32

70x37
52x37
45x37

Barrier Free Shower
(accessible)

Seat
Body Spa
48x48

Alcove
Shower System
60x32

Alcove Shower System
72x43

Claw-foot Tub
66x36

Tub/Shower Combo
65x37

Tub/Shower Combo
60x42
60x33

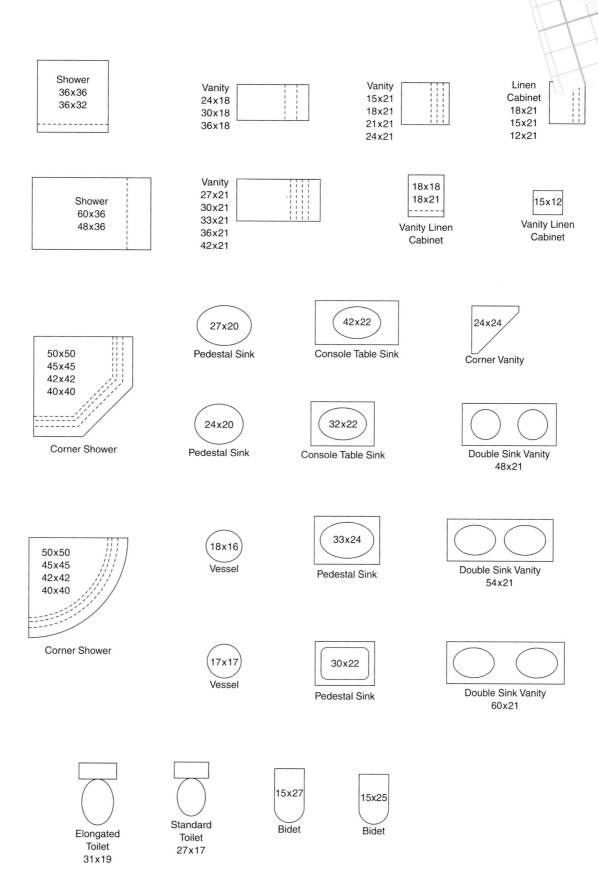

Shower
36x36
36x32

Vanity
24x18
30x18
36x18

Vanity
15x21
18x21
21x21
24x21

Linen
Cabinet
18x21
15x21
12x21

Shower
60x36
48x36

Vanity
27x21
30x21
33x21
36x21
42x21

18x18
18x21

Vanity Linen
Cabinet

15x12

Vanity Linen
Cabinet

50x50
45x45
42x42
40x40

Corner Shower

27x20

Pedestal Sink

42x22

Console Table Sink

24x24

Corner Vanity

24x20

Pedestal Sink

32x22

Console Table Sink

Double Sink Vanity
48x21

50x50
45x45
42x42
40x40

Corner Shower

18x16
Vessel

33x24

Pedestal Sink

Double Sink Vanity
54x21

17x17
Vessel

30x22

Pedestal Sink

Double Sink Vanity
60x21

Elongated
Toilet
31x19

Standard
Toilet
27x17

15x27
Bidet

15x25
Bidet

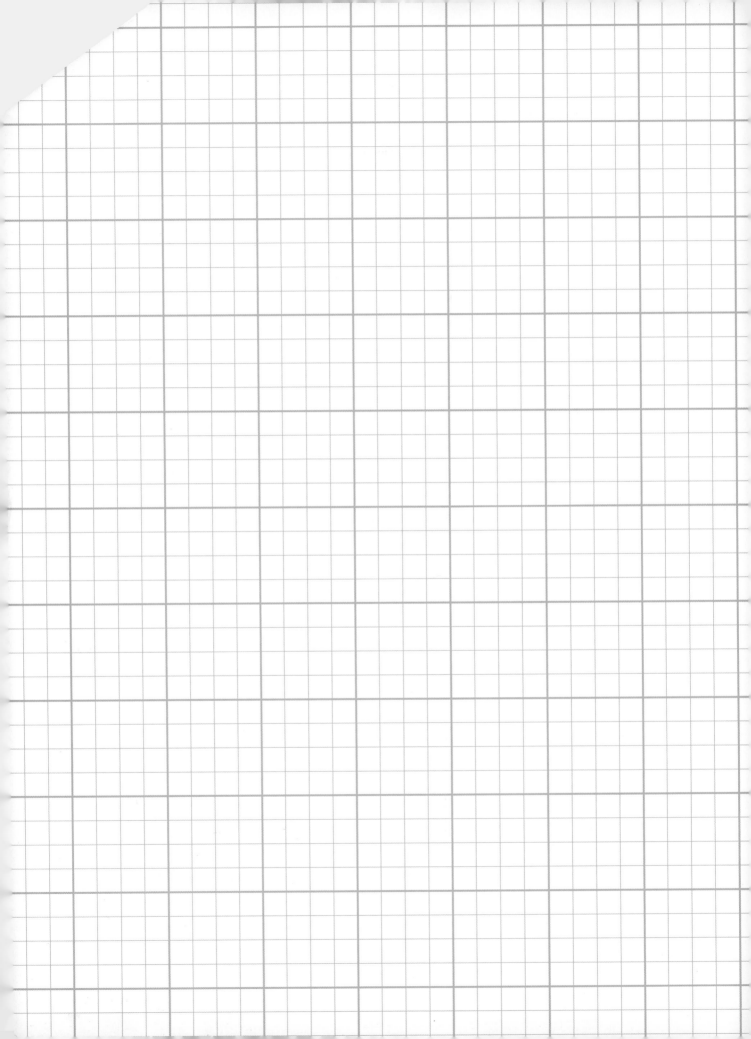

index